Willson's book takes us from his raw, poignantly emotional experience of the death and dying of his parents to an examination of the universal myths that mankind has created since time immemorial to deal with this experience. I laughed out loud and cried while reading his book, and I recommend it as a thoughtful guide to all of us who will not escape this journey.
—Ruth E. Francis, New Mexico Book Association

A thoughtful, powerful, and moving examination of attitudes toward death. Harry Willson uses his own experiences, currently popular beliefs, and mythologies from various cultures to view the subject from many angles. A former scientist and minister, now a humanist, editor, and author, he brings a well-rounded perspective to the subject. Highly recommended to anyone wrestling with the issue of mortality.
—Jon Nimitz, Ph.D., Co-Chair,
New Mexico Chapter Compassion and Choices

This book is provocative reading for anyone who is dealing with death or will face death one day, that is, ALL OF US. Harry Willson examines his personal intense familial experience with death and then proceeds to examine all the myths prevalent in our society that deal with death. Though he has a definite point of view, he does not proselytize. He enables readers to do their own soul-searching. He ends with the notion that each of us can be somewhat responsible for our own exit from the world.
—Rhoda Karp, Hospice social worker, retired

Warning: This book may cause episodes of serious thinking to occur in some readers, especially those over the age of fifty. It could also cause strong re-evaluation of readers' religious understandings, especially in persons who have not allowed themselves to think about and question the stories from childhood and Sunday School.

Harry Willson moves through life thinking, searching and asking the questions we all would ask, if we were brave enough. Searching has produced some answers, which, thankfully, he shares with us in MYTH AND MORTALITY. However, he does not impose those answers on us, because he knows that all of us who give serious thought to these questions will move forward in our own search.

—Shirley Little, Humanist Society of New Mexico

Charles Dudley Warner, nineteenth century author and sometime editor of Harper's Magazine, said, "Everybody talks about the weather but nobody does anything about it." With death we have the reverse: everybody does it but nobody talks about it. [Willson] breaks this silence. He examines death from many angles, assesses the myths surrounding it, and helps his readers think about the subject without fear. He catches and holds interest by stories, including poignant accounts of the deaths of his parents. He gently persuades us that mortality is real; expecting to pass through death to another life is a vain delusion. In doing this, however, he reinforces the truth of a line in Sunday Morning by Wallace Stevens: "Death is the mother of beauty." The fact that our lives come to an end compels us to savor with relish the beauty and good that we experience: flowers, birdsong, starry sky, graphic art, music, love.

—Hershey Julien, Ph.D.,
U.S. representative of Sea of Faith

MYTH AND MORTALITY

TESTING THE STORIES

HARRY WILLSON

Printed in the United States of America
First Printing, 2007
ISBN: 978-0-938513-39-1
Library of Congress Control Number: 2006929562

AMADOR PUBLISHERS, LLC
P.O. Box 12335
Albuquerque, NM 87195 USA
www.amadorbooks.com

This book is dedicated to the memory of the following colleagues and teachers of mine:

J. Paul Stevens
Joseph S. Willis
Lee Huebert
Fred Gillette Sturm

They taught me, by precept and example, that the best way to prepare for the ending of life is to fill life to the brim. They squeezed out every drop.

MYTH AND MORTALITY
A HUMANIST TESTS THE STORIES

Contents

I

TWO DEATHS ONE SUMMER

William Blake believed that if one went deep enough, the personal became the universal. I believe it, too. I intend to go very deep, exposing the personal—it will be up to the reader to determine if anything which approaches the universal has resulted. I recall the young assistant editor who wrote that my topic was not universal enough. She said I had to find something of wider interest and wider application than human mortality. Of course, I realize she wasn't counting the number of people who are mortal. Perhaps she was trying to count the number of people who are willing to think about it.

During the early stages of my life, I was spared direct encounters with Death. My grandparents had died already. Two boys from the neighborhood were killed in the armed forces in World War II, but they were ten years older than I. I watched their parents grieve, but did not miss them, the dead young men, because they had not been close to me.

A six-year-old playmate of my two younger sisters drowned in the creek while I was at high school football practice, and the incident was a serious trauma for my sisters and parents, but somehow Death itself did not touch me.

Elderly persons I had known and loved died while I was away at college and graduate school: the cousin we called "Aunt Mary," who taught me to play the piano; Mr. Mitman, the church elder for whom I had worked on the truck farm for years; Mrs. Hartman, a kind elderly friend across the street. But even all that left me unscathed. I came home for a brief visit, and found one

1

or another simply gone.

The first funeral I attended, I was a pallbearer. I now wonder if that's unusual. My wife's grandfather had died and we went to her home for the funeral. I had not been close to him. The second funeral I attended I officiated. At age twenty-one, I became student pastor of a Presbyterian Church in northern New Jersey. I drove home from seminary in a raging snowstorm in order to conduct the funeral of a man I had never met. I came to know and love that family later, but at that funeral, Death was still distant. The funeral was a type of performance, a sort of test, of me—but Death and I were still not acquainted.

Over the next thirteen years I performed many funerals. When the dearly departed were strangers to me, I read the verses that were supposed to be comforting. I remember being upset over the death of a teenager I had never met, killed in a car wreck. Mostly the funerals were of old people, who had been sick. Death was what followed age and illness, mostly.

The message Christian pastors are charged to deliver deals with Death as though it were part of man's punishment for wrong-doing. Victory over Death is the heart of "the gospel." But a young pastor full of vigor and zeal can get by without feeling much of that. I was more concerned in those days about the deaths in Viet Nam, and what I felt was our collective responsibility for causing them, far more than the Christian message of eternal life, and victory over Death.

The hardest funeral for me was the very last one at which I officiated—a sixteen-year-old favorite of mine, Jeannie, who succumbed after fighting leukemia for several years. Her family persuaded me to preside, even though I had already left the church, in sorrow and anger over that faraway war. My text was from Job: "*The Lord giveth and the Lord taketh away; blessed be the name of the Lord.*" I spat out the last words with venom, not accepting in my heart that the Lord was good or wise or merciful, or that what he had just done was in any way a blessing.

But all that was almost forty years ago. I haven't gone back to the church. My own children are grown and on their own. Many bridges have gone under the water. My sixth book has been published, **Freedom from God: Restoring the Sense of Wonder**. Another manuscript is ready: **The Wonder of Being Old**. It contains some of my musings about this stage of life, and Death.

I don't have to preach at funerals anymore, and it's a good thing, because now I would not be able to quote the old verses without comment, and my comments would reveal my doubts about many things. I'm no longer sure enough of myself to know quite what to say. What I'm inclined to say now, I couldn't have said back then, because I didn't know it, wasn't old enough and hadn't tried on enough elderly people's moccasins.

Several factors contributed to the fact that I was estranged from my parents for more than a decade—not totally out of touch, but not close. My second marriage seemed to cause some of the tension, but mostly it was my renunciation of Christianity and my aborted career as a clergyman. At bottom I now see the problem was my refusal to remain a child.

My father's letters were full of Bible verses, quoted in hopes that I would come to my senses and get back on track. My replies did not help bridge the growing rift. "You cite texts as if you thought I had forgotten some verse, and if only I would remember it, then I would straighten out. The problem is that I know all those texts, in Greek and Hebrew, and have not forgotten one jot nor tittle. You see, I am not a back-slid Christian. I am a post-Christian. I tried that. I did all that. I tested that and found it doesn't work, for me. I have gone on to the next thing. If I were to do what you expect me to do, or hope I'll do, it would feel like a huge step backward for me."

When I left the church I found myself in a precarious mental state. I was feeling that I had spent my entire adult intellectual life, all my professional expertise, on something which had turned out to be a crock of baloney, putting it politely. But that is not a good state of mind to be in. All kinds of nihilism beckon. I was "lucky." I found a job teaching sixth graders, and was free to teach whatever came up, largely. The boys and I spent months—I spent years—studying the myths and legends and fairy tales of the world. We dug into all those belief-system stories, from all over the world. I found Joseph Campbell, ages before Bill Moyers introduced him to the TV audience, and his writings were like food and drink for a starving man. I gobbled it all up, and reread and studied and inwardly digested the myths of the world.

I began to examine my dreams, and formed groups in which together we examined one another's dreams. I read Freud and Jung—all about The Unconscious and archetypes. And I found all the broken pieces, which had been me, coming together at last. I had not learned Greek and Hebrew for nothing. Those Scriptures were the basic texts of a belief system, which was the way to inner truth for many. The claim that it was The Only Way was simply ridiculous in the light of all that study of what the peoples of the world have known and believed for ages, but it could function as one of many Ways. That insight allowed a partial reconciliation with my parents. I could let them have their Way. It was fine, for them, even if not for me.

I tried very hard to "get through," to both my parents, for years, by letter. I stayed away, because of one disastrous visit I made there with my new wife, Adela, early in our marriage. But I kept sharing with them what I was learning, in hopes that they would allow me to be me, and that we could be friends, as adults.

It didn't work. They kept trying to push me backward. They kept treating me as a child. Some of my responses became admittedly a little shrill. "This parent/child relationship is hereby ended, for lack of a child!" They didn't think it was clever, or funny, or true.

One of the dream groups helped immensely. My troubled

dreams, and the patience and love of the people in the group, finally brought me to see that I must give up "that neurotic hope," as a dear friend put it. That hope that I could be an adult friend of my parents, that hope that they'd be interested in my happiness and further growth rather than their "plans and hopes" for me—give that up, and be healed. I did, and went through something that felt like grief, including tears and nightmares. But it became calm inside. The letters in both directions said less and less. But I did not tell them to get out of my life altogether, as I might have. I allowed the kind of relationship they seemed satisfied with. "Since he won't *obey*, we'll keep it cool and keep correct appearances."

The tie was no longer strong and close and binding. I had already gone through grief. I had done all I could, short of *obeying*, which was out of the question, if I was to be a free and responsible adult human being.

I had not been in my parents' home for eleven years. Two thousand miles separated us. My father was eighty-five years old, and had suffered from emphysema for many years, after smoking heavily since he was twelve years old. My mother was ten years younger and in good health. She had fought a tendency to be overweight all her life. She had worked very hard and earned a rest.

My father's illness worsened. A call came from my sister, Sue. He had suffered an embolism—an air bubble in the brain, not unlike a stroke, but probably with no brain damage. He was hallucinating badly, mostly nuclear war stuff.

I decided to go visit, alone, in the midst of a bitter cold winter. I entered the hospital room the evening I arrived. The problem started up immediately. "Oh, my boy came home! Aren't you my little boy?"

"No." My first word was, "No." "I am not a boy. I am a man. I am an *old* man!"

"Oh, well, I didn't mean that."

"That's what you said!"

The visit confirmed my memories of his contrariness. I joined the group which tried to convince him that he must give up driving. "You could have another seizure and hurt someone." "The doctor's gonna fix that." "No, he isn't. It could happen again at any time. It is immoral, and unChristian, for you to drive. You could black out and kill a dozen people." My sister Sue took care of it by talking to the doctor. When he dismissed the old man from the hospital, he wrote a prescription for some medicine. Then on a fresh sheet he wrote a second prescription, which said simply, "No driving."

That settled it. I went out into the cold for groceries, in my father's car, after getting him home from the hospital, and when I returned he greeted me with, "I sold the car." Over the telephone he did it, for a song.

Maybe I tell all this because, if I appear a little contrary and stubborn myself in this story, it's hardly any wonder.

My mother was delighted with this visit, and with another that I made very briefly by bus with a writer friend two summers later. She wanted appearances to be right. The dutiful son comes to see his ailing father from time to time. She and I had quarreled over external appearances long ago. She couldn't believe that I didn't care what the neighbors thought, about anything. Evidently my long absence, and my peculiar life-style, which included divorce, remarriage, periodic job-quitting and career-changing, no visible means of support at all at times, demonstrating a kind of faith in the Cosmos which they would not allow as comparable to their faith in God—all that had made for strange and strained explanations to the neighbors. Now that I was visiting again, everything was all right, they thought. It didn't seem to amount to much, and wasn't all right with me, because Adela wasn't included, but it was as much connection as there was likely ever to be.

During the bus-trip visit Dad came nearest ever to talking about Death. "I don't want to live to be a hundred, like I thought I did." His grandmother had done so.

"Oh? How so?" I asked.

"Life's not that inter'sting anymore."

"Oh," I said, and thought a minute. "I guess not, then," I added. He gave me a funny look, as if that wasn't what he wanted or expected me to say. I had his evaluation of life in mind, later. If he hadn't told me that, perhaps I would have handled him differently than I did.

The following spring another call came from Sue. More embolisms, more general weakness—our father wouldn't last long. I called my mother. "Do you want me to come?"

"I'd rather you came for the funeral."

"Oh. All right. Are you all right?"

"It's rough, but we're makin' it, one day at a time."

"Shouldn't he be in a home? You'll exhaust yourself," I told her.

"I'll be all right. I want to do it."

"O.K."

So, I waited for the news that he had died. I had to chuckle when I realized that what still mattered most to my mother was how it would all appear to the neighbors.

Sue called. Dad was likely to pull out of it for now, even though she had thought he would not. I told her about his sentiments of resignation of the previous summer. She had not heard of them at all. "They're not in his mind at all, evidently," I suggested.

"Nope!" she agreed, quickly and forcefully.

In July she called Adela with news. Mom had died. Sue stopped by early in the morning, on her way to work, and found her on an armless, backless stool against the wall, with her head leaned back against the wall, still warm but dead. There hadn't been enough violence to knock her off the stool. Dad, where he had lain for months on the daybed in the same room, was turned away from Mom, not in his normal position.

I had promised Mom I would go for Dad's funeral! When I called Sue, I could feel her wanting me to come, so I agreed. Ann, my other sister, was reacting more emotionally than Sue or I—"He killed her! He killed her!"

"What does Ann mean?" I asked Sue.

"He demanded too much. Every ten minutes. Day and night. Wouldn't let her turn the light out. She couldn't keep it up. She was exhausted." I learned, in fact, that she had admitted to Sue on Tuesday that she couldn't do it anymore, but when they tried to put him in a home, there was no room. They thought there'd be a place by Saturday. Sue found Mom dead on Friday.

I flew from Albuquerque to Philadelphia and rode up into the Susquehanna West Branch valley with Ann. I arrived at the home I was born in more than fifty years before on a Saturday evening. My sisters, some of our children, some of my grandchildren, friends and neighbors all filled the house. I approached my father in his daybed, and his greeting was, "I think maybe I was too much work for Mother," meaning *my* mother, not his, although he often called her that.

My sisters tell me that that was his first, and only, so far as they know, spoken acknowledgment of her death. His words and that tone suggested that he was expecting in reply something like, "Oh, don't talk like that," or maybe, "Well, she did what she thought she had to do."

Instead, I replied, totally unpremeditated and sounding as Scottish as my mother, very much in *her* tone of voice, "So I hear!" He never brought the subject up again, although I did.

A place was found for Dad in a different nursing home, the day after Mom's death. Payment was required in advance, instantly. My sisters arranged the payments, but then kept him at home, for two reasons. My father was required to attend the funeral. I asked if it was really necessary, and Ann burst out, "Yes! He needs to know what he did!" I subsided. The other reason was that everyone, including me and grandchildren and in-laws and boyfriends—everyone was going to be required to take turns by the hour, according to a written sign-up sheet and schedule which Ann provided, doing what Mom had killed herself trying to do, day and night. Take care of Grandpap.

For the next four days I took my turn, and extra turns, and never relented from what felt like my task. I did not plan it in advance and did not rehearse my lines in any way. I simply continually challenged him that it was *his* move. Everyone reported that he slept seldom, day or night, yet he often appeared to be sleeping when it was my turn to do what Jessie died trying to do. I did not use the time for rest. I spoke to him anyway, allowing for some kind of subliminal hypnagogic effect. "Let go. Let go. Go. Be on your journey."

There had been tension between Mom and Sue, over the care Dad demanded. His infantile need for special attention grew steadily worse. Sue insisted to Mom, "You must limit him."

"It's easier to give in to him than to fight him."

Sue could hardly watch Mom do what she was doing and refused to do it herself.

"Jessie, come make me comfortable," he demanded.

Sue went to him. "What do you need?" He gave her a blank look. "What do you want?" Sue asked.

"I don't want you. I want Jessie." But he didn't need anything, and didn't even have anything particular in mind.

Sue scolded him and warned Mom again, "You must limit him." But her practical ways disturbed Mom.

"Yer faither's daein'!" she blurted in thick Scottish accent.

"Aye, but you be careful, or he'll be the death o' you first," Sue warned, using one of Mom's Scottish phrases.

"How can you say such a thing? Where did you come from?" Mom asked. A taboo hung around the subject for her, it seemed, the subject of dying, and I wouldn't have thought so, but it was true. When Sue told me all this, I was glad Mom didn't have to deal with my retort. It blurted out o' me as Sue repeated Mom's exclamation, "Yer faither's daein'!"

"Aye, 'n why'n't he gi' on wi' it?" I could talk a little Scots, too. But Mom didn't have to cope with that one. She died first. Maybe she knew what she was doing.

An incident during my earlier visit in the cold came to mind. Dad's first night home from the hospital was wakeful for him. He was up several times and got up to stay at 5:00 a.m. He and Mom slept together on that living room daybed, but he had Mom awake most of the night. I had been upstairs, and was awakened by him several times.

I got up early and found him already up, glaring at the kerosene space heater. "It's broken. Bob'll have to fix it." Bob is Sue's husband.

He had turned switches the wrong way, turned it *off*, thank the Powers That Be.

I was furious. I lit it, and then lit into him. "You better leave that thing alone. You'll burn the house down. And you're gonna hafta lie still at night. It doesn't matter if you sleep. You can sleep day or night. But at night Jessie must sleep. She must get that rest. If something happens to her, we're all in trouble, especially you." He gave me a funny look, and so, for that matter, did Mom. I appreciated Sue's later troubles, remembering that incident.

Several times near the end Jessie had tried to find relief. She told Sue she couldn't continue. Plans went into motion to put Dad in a nursing home. Then Jessie pulled the string. "I can't do it. Let's see what happens," and plans for the nursing home were dropped. Maybe she really meant it the last time she put the plan in motion, but in the end she *still* couldn't do it. So she laid down the entire burden. She feared life, what life seemed to be insisting on thrusting upon her—that her husband be put in a home and she live with *that*—she feared Life more than she feared Death.

Sometimes it feels that her fear of what the neighbors would think or say mattered most of all. She slipped away with no violence, at any rate. "We're takin' it one day at a time," she said to me on the phone, not knowing, or not telling, how many days, how few days, there were still to go. She found a way out.

My daughter Mary took her turn at "taking care of Grandpap." Mary is a very competent mother of four and knows about care-giving. "Get me a drink," he ordered, and she got up and did.

"Wipe my eyes," and she got up again and did, removing drops of sweat with a damp cloth.

"Move that blanket."

"Why, Grandpap?" she asked, not getting up.

"Move it. Fold it right."

"Are you cold?"

"No," he declared, shaking his head impatiently.

"Does it bother you?"

"No."

"Then I'm not going to get up and move it just now."

"Mary, you're contrary as a mule."

It struck us all as funny, when Mary retold it, but it revealed still more of what Jessie had had to go through. Sue had heard her mutter, just once, "Shut up, Harry. Just shut up." Without preamble he burst out, when I was there, "I thought I'd be dead by now." Another time he asked no one in particular, "Why doesn't God come and take me?" Another time, sweeping his arm to include all in the room, he said, "I want you all to pray that I will die."

Mom had told me that last one over the phone. "He wants us to pray that he die!" She was having trouble doing it, or even imagining it. Somehow we've been taught to pray that people *not* die—sick people, soldiers, people lost at sea or in mines, whoever. Our myths don't deal much with his situation. I almost called it a strange situation, but have decided that it is not really strange anymore. An old person, through with life, but not dead yet—it is becoming downright common.

Yet I was annoyed with his behest. Once again, as always with him, it was something someone else was supposed to do. "Be dead by now" is passive, *totally* passive, still not something *he* has to do. Something he has to deliberately just up and do—something which is *his* thing, his business, his responsibility.

And I had some difficulty, challenging him to take up his last task, it felt, because I didn't believe *his* myth anymore, and neither did he, it turned out, and we didn't have words and metaphors that could help him at all. I tried the metaphors of a journey—go on, go on through, go on home, cross over. He refused to listen to the idea at all.

I was excused from the night shift, but took a double Sunday morning stint of taking care of Grandpap, while many others went to church. As I entered the living room, he called, "Are we making any progress?"

I looked at him carefully. He appeared a little weaker, perhaps even thinner, although he was literally only skin and bones. He seemed more weary. So I said, "I think maybe so."

Later I wondered about it. He more likely meant did I think he was getting better. He wasn't tuned into the task of getting on with his pending departure, even though it *was* pending. But for how long could he delay it, by sheer willpower and bull-headedness and mulishness and stubbornness? All those descriptions had been used of him earlier in his life, especially by his wife, our mother.

I was unrelenting in laying his one last task before him. "You have one more thing to do, and you're not doing it." I told him he didn't need to worry, as he insisted on doing, about blankets, paper handkerchiefs, or the light on or off, or even suspicious spots on the skin of his legs and bottom.

> You must make your lonesome journey.
> You must make it by yourself.
> Nobody else can make it for you;
> You gotta make it for yourself.

"Go on. Go on a journey. You must go. You know you must. You sang that song so often. You taught it to us. Let go. Go."

I told him his demands for attention didn't have much to do with actual care for his real needs. "You want someone to come over every thirty seconds and reassure you that you haven't died yet. You look afraid."

"*Of course,* I'm afraid!" He was wide awake and indignant.

"How can you be afraid?" I asked. "After all you taught us? All about how God loves you and Christ has prepared a place for you? About how all is forgiven and we go to a better world? Don't you believe all that? What is there to be afraid of?" He gave his head one negative shake, which had always meant not, "No," but rather, "Now we'll leave off talking about *that!*"

Ann tried to tell him that Jessie, our mother, had shown him how to do it. Just lean back and let go of life and go to sleep. It was the one occasion in which I felt I had help in what had become my task. But he would not.

"You must close your eyes, and go," I told him. "You do this journey inside there. Do you see a road?"

He shook his head, "No."

"You're a follower of The Way," I told him. "You always liked that name for it. Now you must go down that road. Away out of this world. We'll be all right. You go on ahead. It's time

now. Close your eyes, and go. Let go, and go." But he would not.
Another time I asked him, "We're supposed to be like Jesus,
right?"

"That's the idea," he said, sounding a little skeptical. Part of
the problem for him was that his adversary knew all the verses,
better than he did.

"He said he came not to be ministered unto, but to minister.
What's your ministry?" We had often discussed the meaning of
that word, twenty years earlier as I was "leaving the ministry."

"Well, I can write those checks!"

"No," I said. "Sue has to write them. Your ministry is over,
now. Now you must leave it all, and go on." He didn't like it. I
suspect, at this later date, that that approach was doomed because
of all his negative feelings about my having left "the ministry,"
that is, professional ecclesiastical status, so long before.

We attended what is called the "viewing" in that part of the
world, at the funeral home in the evening. My mother's body was
on view. The mortician's art was displayed; quantities of lipstick
were altered early on by request. It still didn't look quite right, I
thought. Mouth too firm, and turned down sternly. Fingers not
twitching. I inherited her twitch, and its absence will be a sure
sign that I am dead, as it was in her case.

"Why do I seem to feel so little?" I wondered to myself. Is
something the matter with me? No. I felt it before. I grieved
already. Back when I quit being the little boy. Not so long ago,
really, but before this. We could have been great adult buddies,
but, no.

I'm sorry she didn't get to live a few years on her own, free
of this task. But then who am I to arrange her life, or to resent
what her life consisted of? He took her widowhood away from
her.

I was glad, right in the middle of it, that she didn't have to
hear me exhort him to be about his true business, to get on with

it, to quit stalling, to let go. She would have hated that. We'd have ended up ranting at each other. This peace is better. She knew what she was doing. That's why she didn't want me to come before his funeral. "Yer faither's daein'!"

"Is he? He's hangin' on, it looks to me like. He's deliberately *not* dying! Where's his courage? Let's see it. I see fear and cowardice and whimpering ego. He wants to live forever. He doesn't care who *else* dies!"

Thank the Powers That Be, she didn't have to listen to any of that kind of thing. My sisters and I thought it, and said some of it the evening after the funeral, and that was enough.

In order for my father to attend my mother's funeral, as Ann and Sue insisted, it was necessary that paramedics from the fire department take him to the church, and attend to him while there. "He needs to know what he did," Ann had said, but he seemed mostly unaware, in the church. At one point he barked out, over the soft sweet organ prelude, "Why don't they get on with it?" The paramedic reached over and patted him on the shoulder.

What a sentence! I thought. That's just what I've been saying, inside my head, in imaginary conversations with my mother—"Why'n't he gi' on wi' it?"

After the church service he was taken back home, while we went to the grave side for the final ceremonies. The music and the coffin and the flowers and the limousine ride all reminded me, in a vaguely uncomfortable way, of my distant past as a clergyman. None of it touched me deeply, as one might think the burial of one's mother should.

"They're buryin' yer mither!" Aye, they are. We are. Because she died.

I went to the house, while everybody else was at church waiting for a dinner prepared by the church women for the family. I found a Bible and read aloud the verses my father had slept through at my mother's funeral.

"*Let not your hearts be troubled: you believe in God, believe also in me. In my father's house are many mansions, if it were not so, I would have told you. I go to prepare a place for you. And if I go and prepare a place for you, I will come again, and receive you unto myself, that where I am there ye may be also.*"

I asked him if he believed that, that he was going to be with God, where Jesus was. He gave his head that single negative shake.

"No," I said. "I'll not hush. We need to talk about this. You need to hear this, to pay attention." He closed his eyes. "You hear me?" I asked, raising my voice a little, sounding just like my mother. He opened his eyes again. "O.K.?" I insisted.

"Yes," he said. "Go ahead and read it."

I paged in the book, and then read more of what had been read at the funeral an hour earlier.

"*Who shall separate us from the love of Christ? Shall tribulation, or distress, or persecution, or famine, or nakedness, or peril, or sword? No, in all these things we are more than conquerors through him who loved us. For I am persuaded, that neither death nor life, nor angels, nor principalities, nor powers, nor things present, nor things to come, nor height, nor depth, nor any other creature shall be able to separate us from the love of God which is in Christ Jesus our Lord.*"

Again I asked him if he believed that.

He said, "Yes, I believe that," but I thought he was saying it to shut me up. I did not believe him.

I tried one more time.

"*The Lord is my shepherd, I shall not want. He maketh me to lie down in green pastures. He leadeth me beside the still waters. He restoreth my soul. He leadeth me in the paths of righteousness for his name's sake. Yea, though I walk through the valley of the shadow of death, I will fear no evil, for thou art with me; thy rod and thy staff they comfort me—*"

He interrupted. "The doctor will make me better."

"No, he won't," I said flatly, surprised at my own patience.

"He can't. Nobody can. The time for that is gone. Now you must go through that valley."

He gave that negative shake of his head again and closed his eyes, dismissing me. "You think you'll be the first man who'll live forever?" I asked quietly. He opened his eyes, and shook his head "no" once again, one shake, and closed his eyes.

> Amazing Grace, how sweet the sound,
> That saved a wretch like me.
> I once was lost, but now am found;
> Was blind, but now I see.

They sang that at my mother's funeral. I found it strange that at some level I did believe in Grace, and I was not at all sure that my father did. I wondered what he thought, as they sang it. Maybe he didn't hear it. How can a person say he believes something for eighty years, and then in the eighty-ninth year demonstrate that he doesn't believe it? When the time comes to do it, and not just talk and sing about it, he does not do it.

I don't believe that I'm a wretch, as the song says, but I feel more at home in the Cosmos than my father did. The whole process became an uncanny confirmation of my view of Christianity and mythology and life and death. If he had died a triumphant and victorious Christian death, perhaps I would have had to rethink some things once again. But he did not.

When we arrived home after the dinner at the church, I picked up my father and carried him out the door and down the steps and into Mary's van. He did not weigh eighty pounds. Mary drove us to the nursing home.

"I don't like this," he said.

"I don't like it, either," I admitted.

"Why are we doing it, then?" he asked.

"Because no one can take care of you."

He glared at Sue. "*She* can take care of me!" he declared, not even using her name.

"No, she can't," I stated flatly. "She has a family, a job, and a life to live. It's out of the question." I didn't even look at Sue, but she touched my arm. I never ever considered laying that task on her, and I believe she was grateful.

At the home nurses and orderlies took him away. My sisters and I spent time in the office of the Director of Admissions. We requested no force-feeding and no heroic measures. That would be in the doctor's hands, we were told. Sue was sure the doctor was already in agreement with us. The key phrase would be, "No transfer to the hospital," where the heroic business, and huge expenses, would automatically go into effect.

"He says he wants to die," Sue told the Director, and I let it stand. "He has dozens of people praying that he will die." The Director understood.

We found Dad in his room. I told him, after looking round, "This is a fine place. You can do what you need to do here." The nurses in the room were stunned, I was told later, and Ann felt very uncomfortable. I wasn't noticing. "I don't want you to be mean and unreasonable with these people," I told Dad. "They have a lot of work to do. Be grateful to them for taking care of you. You have work to do, too, there on the inside. You can close your eyes and be on your way, from here."

I thought of introspection, and an exchange the two of us had had about it. I had been trying to share some of what I had been doing, inside there, in my writing and the dream groups and my memories of childhood. "Too much introspection isn't good for you," he wrote to me.

At that time my reply was an angry yelp, "Introspection is not the most important thing. It's the only damn thing." Later I softened a little. If introspection refers to thinking of ego, and ego only, then too much of that is not a good thing. I wondered later, if that was what he meant, but found myself doubting it.

Introspection inevitably leads to thoughts like, "I messed that up."

"I didn't do that very well."

"I wasn't thinking and got it wrong. I'm responsible for what happened, and it makes me feel bad."

My father seldom thought like that, really. He had an uncanny way of finding someone else to blame.

I felt resentment, right there in the nursing home. It seemed to me that remorse and guilt, over what had just happened, would have been enough to do him in, but he felt none. He, who had handed out such quantities of guilt to others, felt none at all, it seemed.

But I wasn't sure of that, either, later. Maybe that was why he was afraid to die. Now God'll really tan his hide, for what he did to Jessie...

"The spirit is willing, but the flesh is weak," Jesus said, when the disciples fell asleep at a time when he thought they should be watching.

"The spirit is willing, but the flesh is too strong!" a fellow told us years later, as his mother's body lingered after her mind and spirit had gone on ahead.

"The flesh is weak, but the spirit isn't willing," I thought to myself as we left the nursing home that late afternoon.

Sue's husband, Bob, took me back to the home next day, so that I could say goodbye to Dad before returning to New Mexico. We found him whimpering. "Why did you let them do this to me?"

"I'm doing it to you, too."

"Why?"

"You can't take care of yourself anymore."

"They don't take care of me here, either."

"Sure, they do. You're warm and clean and dry and fed."

"They don't come when I call," he wailed.

"Oh, of course not," I said. "They have work to do. No one can do what Jessie tried to do. *She* shouldn't have tried. She died, trying."

He seemed to feel, even yet, no remorse over her death. No concern for Pippin, the little dog that supposedly meant so much to him. No concern for Ann or Sue, and their grief over their mother's death. No perceptible concern for me at all—

He reared up in the bed and looked more alert and more purposeful that I had seen him at any time on this visit. He raised his arm and pointed a finger at me and emphasized each word with that finger, declaring, "I want you to move back to Pennsylvania, soon and permanently."

I chuckled, and laughed it off, and said, "Oh, I can't do that. I have my life, and it's out there in New Mexico. We all have our lives to live. We're all doing fine. And you have your journey to take."

He wilted. The conversation languished, and then picked up a little, between Bob and me.

Dad interrupted, and said to me, "Goodbye, then." I looked at him, a little blankly. "Good luck out there, and goodbye," he added.

I chuckled again, grinning at Bob, raising an eyebrow, as if to say, "This is what he's good at." I turned back to Dad and he repeated again, "Goodbye, then."

It was a dismissal. The final dismissal. Obey, or be gone. He's sending me on *my* journey! "Oh!" I cried. "You're being the tough one! Why are you so contrary?"

"Goodbye, then." And it became his only refrain. He said it half a dozen more times, as Bob and I tried to resume the "visit." He would have no more. Just, "Goodbye, then." We finally left, with grim chuckles, Bob and I. He really told me off, and dismissed me, for good. There was no happy noble ending, no reconciliation, at all. Those were his last words to me. "Goodbye, then."

So, those of you who have fathers who approve of you,

rejoice and be exceeding glad. That is, providing that you are at the same time running your own life and not being someone else's representative or appendage.

I recalled my father's unhappiness at the geographical distance between us. He really disapproved of it from the beginning, but he was stuck. Almost thirty years earlier I had gone two thousand miles away, not knowing exactly where I was going, on direct marching orders from the Lord of Hosts. Then after many years of service I ceased believing in the Lord of Hosts, but the distance remained in place. My father did not get unstuck from the notion that the Lord outranked him, until the very end. Then, when it was clear that he didn't believe that stuff either, he was able to say what he'd wanted to say for decades: "I want you to move back to Pennsylvania, soon and permanently." But by then it was ridiculous, and so he was left with, "Goodbye, then."

For me it was the final release. You can't please him. You will not ever please him. So leave off trying, and drop it. "What do you want to be when you grow up, Harry?" the therapist asked me once, when I was in my thirties, old enough to know better than to live my life trying to please Daddy.

It's a tough one. Jessie once told me that Ann was an extension of her. I didn't please her by stating, "Oh, that's too bad. When does she get to be herself?"

Jean Pierre Rampal's mother wishes that the greatest flautist in the history of our species would quit tootling on that darn thing and get serious and go to medical school and become a doctor.

"Goodbye, then."

When I left him in the nursing home, I did not smell Death near Dad. I had been a clergyman long enough to become familiar with that smell, and it was absent. When I left Pennsylvania, I did not believe that he would die soon. He was strong, and contrary. I was sure that his care would take what money there was, and that life would be very difficult for Sue, the only one of the three of us who lived nearby. The cash on hand would last four months. If the house hadn't sold at a fair market price by then, he'd go on Medicaid and stay at the home, with a tally running. When the house sold, the bill at the home would be paid, and the home would continue chewing up the balance. When it was all gone, after two years, more or less, he would stay at the home, with Medicaid picking up the tab.

One week after I arrived home, Sue called. The nurses found Dad in the bed dead at 5:30 in the morning. For my sisters' sake, to make it "clean," I flew once again to Pennsylvania.

What happened as he died? How did my father go? No one knows. I for certain do not know. My journal says that I was restless that night. Sue's call woke me at 5:30 a.m., our time.

Life is like hang-gliding, I notice. You can glide for a very long time. You can catch updrafts and find yourself higher than you were for a while. You can soar and soar. But, finally, you must come down. You can't glide forever. You can land gracefully, before you're exhausted, or you can simply let gravity defeat the exhausted mind and muscles. Either way, you must come down.

Did he crash? I wondered. Did his willpower finally give way before the crushing weight that pulled him down?

I do not know. I'd like to believe that he finally did let go deliberately, and that he knew a moment of surrender and peace as he did it.

More and more I see deliberation in my mother's dying. She knew what she was doing. She quit. She gave up the ghost. Found a way out, and demonstrated at the same time her strange personal fearlessness. Her method seems very abrupt, because we were all concentrating on the long, slow agonizing process of our father.

I had asked Ann, "He hasn't refused to eat?" This was at the time of Mom's funeral.

"No."

"You don't force it on him?"

"Oh, no! But I offer it."

"And he eats."

"A little."

But, then, in the nursing home, for all those old fussy reasons that revealed how spoiled he was all his life, what with that incredibly long list of things he had refused to eat all his eighty-eight years, he did, I'm sure, refuse to eat what they offered him, and thus he did, in ten days, die. I just hope there was a willingness in him.

Remembering all this and recording it, and thinking about it at great length, is doing a strange thing to me. I remained young a little long, that is, psychologically attached to parents. Now I feel that I am turning old a little early, thinking all these heavy thoughts, working on it, chewing on it, like a dog with a bone.

I've had people ask me, "Why are you so concerned about Death?" Or, "Do you think there's any significance in the fact that you're always thinking about dying?"

"These plays of yours, the novels, this myth book—all about Death. What are you doing, Harry? Have you had a personal medical report you aren't telling us about?"

No, nothing like that. But Old Death sits on my shoulder, watching it all. And he hangs around, and makes a formal call, from time to time. A brother-in-law. The butcher next door. A dear friend. My friend's father, and then her mother. But sometimes he wanders off and we think we can forget him. Sometimes he seems several decades early, what with wars and murders and epidemics and what are euphemistically called "accidents." And sometimes it seems he's a little overdue—why all this lingering, in utter uselessness and weakness?

Thinking like this is having an effect on me. I can't get everything done in one day, and I suspect that trying to do so too frantically would bring Old Death into the picture sooner, but I do keep him in my mind. I'm trying to keep life clean and open and honest. He'll interrupt, when he will. I do not intend to let fear of him hinder, or even affect in any way, what we do meanwhile. We'll continue to seek the Heart's Desire.

Meanwhile, it is not morbid to think of Death. It is cowardly and stupid not to.

"So, what do you think?" someone could ask.

I don't like it, some of it. I don't like not being in control of it. I don't like the indignity that is common with it. I don't like the insincere hoverers.

But I do like the infusion of honesty that comes with it. I do like the grim reality of it. I do like Truth.

I felt very little loss at the time of the deaths of my parents. What was to lose had already been lost. Lost and gone forever. I was detached from it all. I was doing all that flying for my sisters' sake, and I think they were glad of it.

My mother's death had come as a surprise. I had done for my father what his pastor might have been expected to do. Helped him die, or tried to. Read Scripture to him. Reminded him of his faith. But I did not baby him. "Be a man, my father." I had no regrets in that regard.

Nevertheless, the philosophical implications of the grim fact of Death itself up close, in the gene pool sense, are heavy anyway. Life is short, even when it's eighty-eight years long. Life is fragile. Life can be squandered, and *is spent*, on one thing or another, a little at a time, at all times, whether we pay attention or not. And then it is all gone.

Tempus fugit. Time flees. "Time flies" doesn't tell it all. Time flees, hurrying away, hastening away from our impotent attempts to grasp and hold it. Time flees. You don't have to kill it, ever. Inexorably it marches quickly on, on and gone. Each new moment is a gift.

ॐ

I wrote poems and recorded memories on the flight east. They lost my luggage on the way—I saw it on the tarmac all by itself as the plane pulled out of a connecting airport. I wrote, in the middle of a heavy page: "Lost luggage is low on a philosopher's list of worries. So cool it." My daughter, Mary, and I had another pleasant four-hour ride together in her van, and we arrived after dark.

The funeral next morning was almost perfunctory. Very few townspeople attended. "It was Mom they liked," I thought. I was struck by what felt like untruths at the church services. The pastor spoke of "Harry's faith," meaning my father's. Maybe he had to. I would have steered clear of that topic myself. I'd have been inclined to emphasize the sovereignty of God, maybe, or the inexorable, undeviating, overarching Justice, wishing a little wistfully, maybe, that I could believe in it myself and consistently act accordingly at all times.

I was feeling heavy. What kind of old person will I turn into? How dictatorial are these genes? Can I do anything about traits in me, that I didn't like in them? Jessie's rant and Harry's thoughtlessness? If I intend to do something, I don't think it should be put off. Old people turn into what they've been all along. Take a good look at this, Harry. Pay attention.

They were singing, "Count Your Blessings." Yes. Excellent idea. I did so, while they sang.

[1] My wife, Adela. I am luckier—doesn't that mean "more blessed?"—than I ever could have imagined, to have her to share the work with, and to find together tenderness and meaning and even cosmic purpose.

[2] My children, who are excellent human beings without having to strain to live up to my expectations.

[3] Health and intelligence.

[4] A kind of caring, or passion, or something, which draws me to people and which they respond to.

[5] Work to do, lots of it, more than I can finish in a normal course.

When I returned home, people here startled me, telling me that my father had done what I told him to. He let go. It only took him twelve days to do it. He got through. He crossed over. Perhaps the process was not as long and drawn-out in reality as it seemed to me to be.

All that was twenty years ago. Since then I have been working on this book. It seems to me that it would be helpful if we humans thought more carefully and more extensively about death. My mother surprised us all by dying, when she did and the way she did. And my father's way of handling it indicated, to me at least, that the stories and myths we've been using need to be reconsidered.

At first I called my book, **Myths to Die By**, mimicking a title Joseph Campbell used, **Myths to Live By**. What stories and images and metaphors do we use among ourselves, we humans, to help us deal with the fact that we are mortal?

My original title would never do, I realized, since most of my intended readers would be put off by that. The majority of humans do not want to think about dying.

But life has a way of insisting sometimes, so I persisted. I began to list all the stories I could find, and then began to evaluate them. Some may be more helpful than others. I evaluate them from a humanist perspective. Science and reason, good sense, and common sense, rather than irrational authority, will be our guides.

ﮯﮯﮯ

II

THE DENIAL OF DEATH

Ernest Becker wrote a book back in the 1960's entitled, **The Denial of Death**. His thesis is that culture itself is created by psychological repression and that the content of that repression is refusal on our part to accept our mortality. He believes that this happens in all cultures. The purpose of the culture, primitive or modern, is to deny the fact of death. Those rare individuals who don't go along blindly with the lie which denies our mortality are out of step with whatever culture they are living in.

Becker, like many European and North American writers, may be extrapolating too much from our culture to "all cultures," but his book is extremely provocative, more so now than when he first wrote it. Our own culture, which is the one he is really writing about, is extremely confused, and the way we deal with death makes Becker's thesis relevant to our daily lives.

Jessica Mitford wrote **The American Way of Death**, which describes the funeral customs of our culture. Elizabeth Kubla-Ross wrote several books about dying, and "death and dying" has become an encyclopedia category, and a subject for many subsequent books, including this one.

The hospice movement has been revived, in which religious groups prepare individuals for the inevitable. This is a hopeful trend, reversing the denial which is typical of most religious enterprises. Indeed, denial hovers over almost every aspect of human existence in our culture.

A debate about doctor-assisted suicide rages in the media and the courts. This debate is totally inappropriate at this time, since we have not yet established a system of universal health care. Before that is done, cost accounting will inevitably take precedence over science, ethics, morals, fairness, theology or any other consideration.

As a culture we seem to be talking about death nowadays more than we did when Becker proposed **The Denial of Death**. Perhaps this is an illusion of mine, caused by my advancing age. Yet I suspect the falsehood he spotted is still alive and influencing how we think and behave. To a large extent we are still denying the simple fact of our mortality. Our culture is confused, on a grand scale.

There has never been a nation more obsessed with the preparation of instruments of death on a mass scale and at the same time so inadequate in the preparation of individuals for the experience. After sixty years of preparation for mutually assured destruction, our national leaders still prate about and plan for deaths in the dozens of millions, and argue among themselves as to how many such deaths are "acceptable." For a while there was no enemy in sight worthy of the quantity of hostility or expense involved in this effort, yet our government continued to prepare the materials and instruments which are enough to ensure the extinction of the process of life itself on this planet.

Now there is an enemy, but the new war is not aimed at an enemy but at a tactic. "Terror" is a tactic which appeals to the desperate and the insane. A "war on terror" will be never-ending, since there is no defined enemy to defeat, and no way to define victory. It becomes, then, a rationale for permanent war and an ever-escalating war budget. And yet only a tiny minority of our people participate in any real objection to this death obsession of the government.

For a short while the talk was that the budget would be reduced after the end of the Cold War, but it wasn't. The ingenuity of the vast majority of our scientists is still dedicated to weapons of mass annihilation. Upgraded nuclear weapons, and biochemical weapons as such, have not yet been denounced and scrapped, but instead consume an ever larger proportion of the national military budget. Denial is widespread. Experimentation on unknowing citizens in the field of "nuclear medicine," in ways that remind one of Auschwitz, has been denied even in the face of exposure, and is still not being dealt with frankly. Denial has been the pattern in analyzing the effects of Agent Orange, and in even defining what is called Gulf War Syndrome and its possible causes.

At the same time our people are unprepared for dying. The vast majority refuse to think at all about the megadeaths the leaders are preparing and denying. For the most part they also procrastinate about thinking about their own individual departures. That subject creates great uneasiness but is seldom talked about frankly.

We are in the midst of two epidemics, either of which could be compared to the Black Death of the Middle Ages. According to statistics, cancer will take one fourth of us, sooner or later. Most of our scientific effort is dedicated to finding a cure, while prevention is largely ignored, even though there is some clear knowledge about the causes of cancer. Tobacco kills more than a thousand persons per day, mostly from one form of cancer or another. Industrial and internal-combustion-engine pollution are known causes, but the corporations have silenced or purchased the scientists, for the most part.

AIDS has now reached into every community in this country, and in the long run we will have to deal with it in a rational and, hopefully, kind manner. Much of the entire continent of Africa is at risk. Some skeptics wonder where the virus came from in the first place, and wish it could have become enough of a *cause celebre* to blow the secrecy lid off the biological warfare laboratories of our own government, but so far it has not. Anthrax research appears to be another tip of this same iceberg. In any case, these two epidemics, cancer and AIDS, may yet force us finally to think about Death, much as we wish it otherwise.

Of course, the denial of death, no matter in what culture we find it, does not really work. Every human being, no matter who denies and how much, finally dies. With the elderly infirm, in our culture, our custom is to wait for death, or "God," to come and take away the one racked with pain, weakness, frustration and perhaps fear, while our efforts at care and the impressive accomplishments of the medical profession sometimes prolong the departure beyond everyone's endurance. Death is delayed, through all our efforts, and sometimes with an assist from the willpower of the dying one. We do not have much tradition that tells of confronting death and planning for it and allowing it and accepting it and going to meet it.

My father's last days were a clear instance of the denial of death. "The doctor's gonna fix that," he kept insisting, even after it was perfectly plain to everyone else that the doctor was going to do no such thing.

When he did speak of his own death, he was consistently laying some task on other people—that we should pray, and that "God" should take action. My challenge to him to take up his last task willingly and quit resisting the inevitable amounted to my wish that he would cease the basic denial.

In contrast, my mother seems to have confronted Death directly. I can imagine her last conscious moments. "I'm too tired. I can't do it anymore. I'll just rest here." And on her backless stool she laid her head back against the wall and gave up the ghost.

Yet she, too, had been in another sort of denial. The topic of Death verged on the realm of taboo. There was hush and mystery in her voice, when she said, "I'd rather you came for the funeral." And again, "We're taking it one day at a time." When she broke through the taboo barrier, it was to scold. "Yer faither's daein'!" We were all supposed to respond in a sort of awe, and when my sister didn't, Mom was more upset than ever. There was denial at the heart of her attitude.

Other cultures prepare people for Death, better than our total lack of such traditions can possibly do. Many of the world's myths say that humanity as a whole, through a character who represents us all, chose Death one way or another.

The Blackfeet tribe tells one which describes First Woman and the Creator talking. The Creator took a buffalo chip and suggested tossing it into the water. If it floated mankind would live forever, but if it sank, humans would live a while and then die. First Woman, grossly inexperienced, having been created just that same morning, said, "Oh, no. The buffalo chip will come apart in the water. Here, let's do it with this stone." The Creator agreed, and of course the stone sank, and thus our fate is to live a while and then die.

A tribe in New Guinea tells that humans were given the choice of whether they wanted to be like the snake or like the bird. They chose the bird, who can fly. It was too bad, the story says, because they passed up the opportunity to be like the snake, who sheds his skin periodically and lives forever. Instead humans are "Dead Birds," which is the title of the Michael Rockefeller documentary film which includes this tale.

The myth from the Fertile Crescent, which is in our Bible, also says that humanity chose death. The stories from the Blackfeet and New Guinea suggest that we chose out of ignorance, but the Biblical view insists there was some contrariness in it, too. The Creator warned, "In the day that you eat of it—that fruit of the knowledge of good and evil—you shall surely die." But Eve, and then Adam, ate anyway, and Death was the result.

The fact that this realism about Death is in the Bible does not mean that a practical acceptance of Death now constitutes part of our tradition. On the contrary, Christian teaching, derived from later parts of the Bible, states clearly that Christ's sacrifice on the cross overcomes, or *undoes*, the consequences of that First

Disobedience, giving believers "victory over Death," thus setting up the very denial which concerns us here. It is curious that it was the serpent, in the role of Tempter, who contradicted God in the original story, saying, "Ye shall not die." Our culture has been believing him, in spite of all the evidence to the contrary. I spoke about mythology at a writers' group, and a middle-aged attendee asked me why I was so interested in mythology. "What is it really all about?" she wanted to know. I told her that I thought it was our mortality. Her reluctance to pursue that topic was quite remarkable.

On another occasion, at a science fiction convention, I stated, as a panelist, that I believed all mythology was triggered by the fact of our mortality. A well-known fan of Sci-Fi writers, and scientist himself at the local weapons lab, pooh-poohed the whole idea of mythology, saying that we would soon be solving that problem.

"What problem?"

"The problem of death. Science will overcome that."

He thought that humans, aided by science, will soon cease to be mortal. I've watched plenty of denial on many occasions and in many places, but this one seemed to be an extreme case.

I have observed the effect on me and my mood and my outlook on life, brought about by the task of preparing this book on our mortality. I write, and rewrite and rearrange all this, and read everything connected to this subject, and the result is that I feel more alive, more aroused somehow. I sense the philosophical truth about life, about living, about being who I am. I sense more clearly than usual that I am a breath, a wisp, a fleeting thought, a dream—of *almost* no significance at all, part of a huge ancient blinking on/off process, not as special and unique as Ego keeps suggesting. But with that kind of awareness I am able to *be* whatever it is that I am, just be that, and no more. Paying attention to dying makes me feel more alive meanwhile.

Constant fretting about the tasks that I take on, and puzzling over their meaning and wondering about the evaluation others make of my life, can never make me feel more alive, but this awareness of Death can and does.

Some of the reading I've been doing about Death has done me a world of good. **The Hospice Movement**, by Sandol Stoddard, encouraged me greatly, and introduced me to a medieval tract called, **Ars Moriendi**, Latin for, "The Art of Dying"! Dying is an art, a skill, one of the things we may yet have to learn to do. I say, "may," because in our time, and in any other, Death can make a very sudden and unexpected approach—on the freeway, at Ground Zero, at the wrong end of an attack machine gun, in the middle of a cloud of poisonous gas. But, if we're spared all that, and end up weak and weary and worn out and finished with life, then we will still have dying to do. **Ars Moriendi** suggests that we can learn how to do it, and need to learn how to do it.

Ars Moriendi also suggests that we can help each other. In its charming antiquated language the book quotes what the prophet Isaiah did for King Hezekiah. "For when the king lay sick and upon the point of death, he [Isaiah,] glosed him not, nor used no dissimulation unto him, but plainly and wholesomely aghasted him, saying that he should die." What a phrase! Try wholesomely aghasting someone sometime.

I found myself doing exactly that for my father, unpremeditated and unplanned and totally unrehearsed: "You have one more thing to do and you're not doing it... You're stalling... You have work to do, inside there, with your eyes closed... Do you intend to be the first man to live forever?" Overhearers at the time, and hearers and readers of my subsequent telling of it, do not exactly approve, I find. Perhaps they wish I'd "glosed him," kidded with him, pretended with him, lied to him. They note "your hostility toward your father." But it was not hostility. It was detachment, at worst. I think it included a kind of filial loyalty to truth.

ও⋆

Many people are put off from the task of thinking about this seriously, because their experiences with death and the mythology our culture uses have revealed so much insincerity. I'm referring to the funeral rituals in use in our culture. Most of those rituals still belong to the Christians, or were derived from the Christians. A grave in a garden, which is still most typical, comes from that tradition. The presiding official, usually, is a Christian clergyman, who may or may not have known the deceased, and may or may not have a close relationship with the survivors. Presiding at the funerals of strangers is one of the things that Christian clergyman have to do, from time to time. In recent times some have made a business of it.

For practicing Christians, the funeral used to take place in the church building. Nowadays, even for them, and certainly for most other people, the funeral ritual is more likely to take place in a "chapel," which is a Christian-looking imitation of a church, in a mortuary.

All too often there is a kind of built-in hypocrisy, with comments about the faith of the deceased, or the good works, while those who knew that person sit and marvel. One senses an ignorant, even if well-intentioned, groping for comforting phrases, based on generalities and half-baked theology. This is part of the reason so many people "hate funerals," in addition to the unpleasant reminder they give us of where this road of life is leading.

The viewing, with the mortician's craft on display—with lipstick, hairdo and formal clothes, along with the flowers, music, words at the grave side—all these rituals are sometimes simply foisted on the survivors, with or without meaning.

Some unbelievers, or outright disbelievers, want no ritual at all for themselves, or for those they are responsible for. They do not attend other persons' funerals, and have specified, "No memorial service of any kind," for themselves. Whether it's intended or not, such an attitude expresses a cynical isolation, as if to say, "One more mortal human died like a dog." Such a lack of ritual proclaims that the deceased lived for and by himself only and now he's gone, whether it's true or not.

We know a lady, who was married to an outspoken atheist for sixty years, who asked her daughter to arrange a memorial service after her own death, "just in case." It was something of a dilemma. A clergyman, complete with sanctuary, was selected and the family assembled. The memorial part was later counted as "all right," but the Christian sermon and subsequent altar-call were not. The entire incident emphasized the fact that our culture is confused, and that thinking and talking about all this in advance would be a good idea.

We need to be inventing new rituals. In the case of weddings, more and more couples are writing their own vows, when they know that they neither believe nor intend to execute the traditional Christian promises of ownership and obedience. But we have been much less open and prepared in the case of funerals. Simply refusing to have any kind of public family or community acknowledgment that a life has ended is hardly enough.

There is an important function for a funeral ritual of some kind. Some kind of public statement that this life was lived and is now concluded can be very helpful. It serves as a way of saying that we assembled survivors cared about this person and still care about each other. We recognize that this happens to each of us, eventually. We are part of a group. We are a group.

Some kind of ritual needs to express all that. There are some old metaphors available, and we need to feel free to invent some new ones: the river, the sea, the planted tree, the journey, the recorded memory, the interconnected web, the compost pile. We need fresh imagination.

I recall a friend's memorial service. It was held in the chapel of a mortuary, but presided over by her son, not a religious functionary. A large group of friends, many of whom knew each other through her, crowded into the gathering, where, without a formal "Order of Service," each of us took turns saying what we felt and remembered. It became a kind of celebration of her remarkable life. At the son's home afterward, an even more festive mood was felt, which is what she had specified that she wanted—food, her favorite music by The Tijuana Brass, photo albums, with her own handwork on display.

Perhaps we who are still living can mature beyond the denial of death. My friend tells the story of the death of her father. He and his wife were both in their nineties, living in their own home, visited regularly, daily, by several of the grown offspring. The old man had poor vision and poor hearing. He had said that he no longer wanted to live to be a hundred. He was ailing, and they all knew it; he had no appetite and a little fever.

He did *not* want to be taken to the hospital again. He believed, and all his family agreed, except one daughter, that he'd get as good care, and more attention, there in his own home. One daughter wanted him taken to the hospital, no matter what, but the others refused to force him. That same daughter spoke of the future in some connection, but the old man interrupted her, saying, "No, I won't be here. I'm ready for rest, ready to be gone. I'll be gone."

The woman grabbed her father by the shoulders and shook him and yelled, "No more of that! No more talk like that! Who'll take care of mother?"

Not that he was taking care of his ninety-three-year-old wife—she and the daughters were taking care of *him*. It was a refusal to deal with Death, on the daughter's part. The others let it ride, and regretted it later. The desire on that sister's part to put him in a hospital was her intent to put Death off, to let it happen somewhere else and be someone else's responsibility. The doctor had plainly said that the old man would not be better off in hospital, and the whole family recalled that when he *was* there, he was worse off because of inattention from the over-taxed staff.

Tension mounted, mostly about the hospital. My friend prepared lunch for all, including visitors. Her father would not eat. At last everyone left, so the old folks could nap. My friend left to do some of her own work in her own home, which is often neglected at such times. Shortly thereafter she received a guilt-slinging phone call from the irate sister, shrieking that the father had died, and it was all *somebody's* fault.

The mother told the story of the last scene. The old man rose from his nap, wanting to go to the bathroom. He wanted his robe and cane. He started for the bedroom door and stopped. "We have to go across the hall," his wife reminded him. He backed up and sat back, collapsing on the foot of the bed. "What's the matter?"

"I just wish somebody would tell me that it's all right to die!" he wailed. Then he fell back onto the bed full-length, and died, anyway. Since then my friend and I have both concluded that it is in no way a loving act to hinder that departure for someone, or to refuse to talk about it, or plan for it.

ça ça ça

III

OUR AGING POPULATION

Ours is a culture based on the irrational supposition that Death is not real, that the weapons of megadeath will not be used, so it is all right to pay for the preparation of even more of them, and that we have no real responsibility for each other or even for ourselves. It is a strange irony that our culture, which is extremely adept at the denial of death, is also rapidly aging. We have new problems that former societies, for one reason or another, didn't have, and many of those problems have to do with the radical increase in the number and proportion of our population which is elderly. Obviously, it is time death was allowed into our thinking and planning.

Some of the statistics about our aging population are quite shocking. Two-thirds of all the men and women who have ever lived beyond the age of sixty-five in the entire history of the world are alive today. That statistic is from the Age Wave Institute, quoted in **The Washington Spectator**. One-tenth of our nation's thirty million senior citizens have children who are now themselves senior citizens, age sixty-five or over.

Many of those elderly expect someone else to fend Death off for them. But no one can do that. It would be better to face it. And a fair number of the middle-aged expect the elderly to go away with no expense or botheration to them. It does not always happen that way either. If nothing else, the topic certainly needs talking about, in advance.

We know a sixty-five-year-old lady who is selling her

ninety-year-old mother's house and land, for cash, so that she can place her mother in Presbyterian Hospital for terminal medical care at a cost of several thousand dollars a month. The lady and her husband thought they were going to inherit something, but they're not. The hospital will get it, for taking care of the old lady. They were thinking of the house and land as already theirs, in some sense, kind of like inheriting in advance, but no. One can't continue losing sleep and taking abuse and doing extra labor until one's own health fails. So the "inheritance" goes to the hospital, and they'll take care of all that.

We know another woman, age forty, who is still doing what the woman who is selling her house can't continue to do. She sleeps in a chair by the bed, gets up all night, takes horrible abuse, does extra work all the time—for her mother-*in-law*. Everyone wonders whether Death will intervene in time. He doesn't always. Death can play mean in the second half.

For many decades there was a generation between that Great Adventure and me. One's parents are like a psychological buffer between our lives and Death. It isn't necessarily so, but we assume that the parents will die first. It doesn't really even make sense, but it's as if they were protecting us somehow, by living still. When they're gone, the buffer is removed, the screen is torn away and there you are, face to face, momentarily, from time to time, from now on, with Death. That has happened to me and I want to be thoughtful, and truthful, about it.

When we're children, we believe that our parents are the whole world. Growing up consists of finding all the rest of the world out there, "going outside," relating to "the gang," which was not a technical term nor an evil incantation, in my childhood, but simply the word used to refer to my peers outside the family. Growing up was going to school, learning to care about other folks, discovering outsiders, finding tasks and duties and challenges and desires, and dealing with all that.

Some adult children blame their parents for all their troubles and unhappiness, harking back to things that happened decades ago, but they are behaving as little children, allowing too much importance to the parents. Sometimes, when the parents die, the world of the dependent child is shattered, even if the child is middle-aged.

Some middle-aged offspring feel relief, a sense of freedom, when the parents die. It's a sure sign that they have gone through a period of allowing the parents too much power. I know about that, from personal experience.

And sometimes the long drawn-out death-process, with all its misery and expense and gore and mess, can wean the middle-aged child. "I'm ready now for Mom to go," one told me, and she hadn't been until just lately.

In some ways one's elderly parents can keep one from confronting one's own personal mortality. "Dad will fix it," we think. "What are you yourself going to do about it?" we finally have to ask ourselves, when the question does come up at last. Your parents could do nothing to change it, the doctors can do nothing, really—"You die anyway." And sometimes the survivor is furious at the Cosmos for decades, for arranging things this way, and then at last that person can accept How It Is and get over it, and have a few moments to be really alive.

There is a growing awareness of aging in our population, because more and more of us are surviving longer. Sometimes it seems the concern is centered exclusively around monetary questions, like the Social Security Escrow fund. Other matters could be considered, however. The aging process allows time for us to ponder what we know and believe about life, and Death. I'm suspicious of certainty, but I think it is high time we thought about all this seriously and at some length.

I'm not all that old, yet I'm feeling something. Less energy, more morning aches and pains, more sense of time running faster and faster and then running out. Getting old, with grown grandchildren and missing teeth, and less myopia and more arthritis in the neck and fingers, and skin cancer on the backs of both hands—and I find my view of time and tasks is changing. I don't have to, and indeed I cannot, go back and redo much of my life. I can let all that go now, because I have to. I must go on, that's all.

Getting old, for me, means getting at it—whatever it is. Doing it, if I'm really going to. Getting it done, while life and time are allowed in which to continue. Not putting it off any longer. No more procrastination. I tell myself, if you're not doing it, you're not going to do it. If you're going to do it, *now* is the time.

An old friend writes that there will be no more clippings, for his friends or for himself. He has been a very efficient "reader's service," giving me two more eyes, more insight, and additional information. He cannot go on, he says. He's too old. His hand trembles, and the news has no importance anyway. He has aged, gone past that preoccupation with the momentary, which is what the "news" is.

It made us sad. I called and told him so. He said he was not sad. "Just recognizing some facts of life." What a phrase! "The Facts of Life!" That used to mean *birth* and what precedes it. Now it means *death* and what precedes it.

I've been at the task of writing this book for twenty years. I first wrote, "I'm not all that old," some years ago. After that I proposed a column for our local "alternative" newspaper, and the plan was accepted. I wanted the column to be called, "The Longer Perspective," but when the twenty-something kids who ran the paper put it out, my column was called, "The Old Guy." At first I felt less old than that, but gradually I have found the label fitting.

And since then prostatitis has kicked in and made me feel even more of that "old guy" business. "No cancer!" the oncologist shouted all over the clinic, but it makes a body thoughtful nevertheless. And it makes the time left, much or little, more obviously precious.

I wish I could get older people to share more of their insight with me. Not only is youth wasted on the young, but age is sometimes wasted on the old. They have that time in which to think, and all too many of them waste it watching television and berating adult offspring. They have that perspective on life's events, and some of them refuse to think about it and seem to resent *my* wanting to think about it and question them about it. They have some clues to the meaning of life, but some of them don't seem inclined to share. One would think that the approach of Death could diminish the power of Ego. The Ultimate looms—The All draws near—The Melting Down begins. But Ego remains intact, in a good many cases.

My recent observations indicate that old people become more and more what they have been all along. We move more slowly, have less expendable energy, feel more pain and weakness than we used to, as the body coasts downhill past its prime. My wife and I are in close contact with quite a remarkable assortment of people older than we are, and we find ourselves aging gradually, also, with a growing amount of awareness that that *is* what is happening to us.

I don't remember this being talked about so much when I was young. Old people fascinated me, but I don't remember much being made of it. Geriatrics, gerontology, "death and dying"—we have names for things now. But perhaps no less denial.

It is becoming clear that many, perhaps most, perhaps the vast majority, of humans do *not* become wiser as we age. If we did, this would be the Golden Age of Humanity, given those statistics cited above. A quick glance around indicates that such is not the case.

The elderly are not respected in this culture, as they have

been in others, and it is fair to ask, "Why not?" You don't get respect automatically simply by not dying, and you don't get it by lolling around in a semi-conscious mental state mouthing slogans. You don't get respect simply by doing what you're told for six or more decades. You don't get respect by clutching at every dime that comes your way, clinging for dear life to every penny, in a state of total distrust.

Fear of pain, fear of dying, fear even of glancing briefly at the plain fact of mortality including one's own—these things do not lead others to respect, or even care at all about, our views and opinions on life and history and memory.

Elderly persons need to be led into philosophy and contemplation and meditation. Instead they are lied to, fought over, betrayed by the megadeath leaders, and terrorized by fear of pain, fear of want, fear of abandonment and fear of annihilation.

I have come to believe that to the degree that I can at all control what kind of person I am—patient, kind, loyal, truthful, generous—*now* is the time to do that. Aging will erode away pretense and unsubstantial appearances. What's really *in* there is what will show. So be what you are, I tell myself, as if I had any choice. What you are now is what you will be. You won't automatically turn into a better person later, some other day, if that's what you're planning on. Talk about the unexamined life being not worth living! *Now* is the time to do the examining and the deciding and the adjusting and the changing. Many persons who have observed the dying while caring for them have stated that people die the death they have prepared for all their lives. If that's so, now is the time to do some preparing.

I believe in what could be called "truth-in-dying." Simone de Beauvoir, Jean Paul Sartre's partner, wrote a book about the death of her mother, entitled, **A Very Easy Death**. It contains the existentialist non-acceptance of death, but that non-acceptance is made more difficult by all the lying. Two middle-aged sisters lead their elderly mother to believe she will recover, while they know she won't. They never use the word cancer, even after surgery. Unhelpful "religious" meddlers want to, and they try to tell the truth about the old lady's dying, to her, in order to get at their theology, which is almost certainly preposterous and unkind and untrue.

The old lady laments that she will not see Simone again, so Simone returns to Paris from Prague, intending to please her, but with this thought in her mind: "Why attribute such importance to a moment, since there will be no memory?" This may be the key, which allows all the lying. Since there will be no memory, why not lie? Then, why not lie some more? Even the title of the book, **A Very Easy Death**, is a lie.

I find I want truth, in my dying and in anybody's, simply for love of Truth itself. The experience is too important to be got through pretending. "The doctor's going to fix it."

"I'll get better."

"You're doing fine, looking better."

"Promise me you'll return to the church." No, no promises. Isn't that truth better than any lie?

Evidently my allegiance to Truth, just because it *is* truth, and my horror of Pretense, having done enough and too much of that already, are stronger than anyone's undependable certainty about there being "no memory." Don't lie to me, please. Even if I'm in a coma, don't lie.

ϿⱥϿⱥϿⱥ

IV

WE NEED A MYTHOLOGY

My father lay on his deathbed. His demands for care, every five minutes, day and night, had brought my mother to her grave and wore out everyone's patience. I said to him finally, "All you want is someone to come and assure you that you haven't died yet. You look afraid."

"Of course I'm afraid," he said.

"How can you be afraid, after all you taught us? That God loves you and Christ has prepared a place for you? That all is forgiven and we go to a better world? Don't you believe that? What is there to be afraid of?" He would not talk about it.

I sighed. When I turned away from him and left the room I said, to no one in particular, "His mythology let him down."

The phrase was misunderstood, as an attack by me on fundamentalist Christianity. I was not intending that at the time. I was using the word "mythology" technically, meaning "belief system, with all its supporting stories."

My father had believed Christianity all his life, or so he thought and so he led others to think. He believed it, and taught it to us, his children, and we believed it for decades, until our experiences and thoughtful reconsideration made it no longer possible for us to believe it, at least in the same terms in which it was taught. Seeing that mythology fail him utterly in his last days was very disturbing.

I had lost my faith earlier, because of things that happened to me, and because of my search for answers that were consistent with each other and my reality. I wondered when he lost his. I wrote a poem:

> His mythology let him down,
> And I'm not surprised.
> It let me down, too,
> Not when I was confronting Death,
> But when I was trying to figure out
> What Life was all about.

Humans can arrive at a belief-system by carefully examining their received tradition, then thoughtfully pondering their experiences with the hard knocks of life. It requires paying attention to one's own life, examining it with painstakingly careful reasoning. Or humans can end up with a belief-system by default, not having bothered to think about it very much. Either way, that which guides and motivates our attitudes and our actions is a mythology.

The great religious traditions of mankind have provided huge quantities of theologically precise analysis, while at the same time dozens of not carefully thought-out notions serve as part of those same traditions, making much use of miracle stories and tales of the supernatural. Theology or miracle-story—it is all mythology. This is true of Christianity and Judaism and Buddhism and Taoism and Islam, and other systems which are usually labeled "primitive."

"God," in all the traditions, is a myth, a metaphor. True believers do not like the sound of that and become angry at mythologists. The word "myth" puts many people off, even after Joseph Campbell's work became so popular. Many people still use the word "myth" as a synonym for "untruth, lie, falsehood."

It may help to know that even Science, with all its rigid rationalism, can also be called a mythology in the sense used here. Scientists have to use mythological language, after all, to be able to talk about dim beginnings, unimaginable times and distances, and purposes.

We all depend on mythology all the time. Even the most hard-nosed realist/materialist develops an attitude, a point of view, a sweeping perspective and a leap of faith, or *un*faith. That has to be called mythology, too. All of us use metaphor to refer to the world, ourselves, our lives, each other and the process we are in the middle of. That also is mythology.

Our mythology reveals our values, our beliefs, our collective desires as a culture and as a species. The stories we read and tell, the films we see and hear, the poems and songs and jingles that we sing, especially the ones that go rattling in our heads when we're not thinking, the metaphors we use for living and dying, beginning and ending—all that is our mythology.

Many people are glad, and I am one of them, that ours is a pluralistic society. No omnipotent power is dictating yet the one single myth that everyone must live and die by these days, strangling or burning the unbelievers. But the other side of that freedom is that we are left with the task of forming our own myth, and deciding for ourselves.

If we aren't working on our own belief and value system, our personal mythology, a very powerful default factor comes into play. There are myths floating around, many preposterous, many of deleterious effect. Some are flying on very powerful vehicles, like television networks. Many are designed to affect your behavior, especially your spending of money. The subliminal power of all that myth may suck the unaware into a mythology which doesn't work or is unworthy of its adherents.

If we neglect to form a myth, and make it really our own, we'll be living unexamined lives. If we choose to ignore this entire matter, we may run the risk of dying in great perplexity, as my father did. Getting past life's conclusion was extremely difficult for him and troubled the surviving family a great deal.

Not everyone is up to the task of forming his or her own mythology. It's a huge task. The temptation is to turn it over to someone, anyone, who has easy, pat answers to life's questions. That's why cults are so appealing, and why the fundamentalist wings of all the world's major religions have become so powerful and dangerous.

Old persons, who are weary of thinking for themselves, or never tried it, as well as young persons who haven't learned yet how to think at all, become zealots ready to follow leaders wherever they lead. They are ready to follow illogical inferences from simple-minded erroneous axioms into preposterous nonsense. This is the origin of the war mythology which underlies gross criminality and justifies lying, arson and mass murder. For lack of a worthwhile myth much misery results.

There's no question the word "mythology" has been contaminated. For all too many, if "myth," doesn't mean simply, "lie," or "falsehood," it refers to "fairy tale belief suitable for imaginative children." But the original Greek word, *muthos*, meant simply, "story."

We have to be careful, even here. For some the word "story" also simply means "lie." Where I live we're mixing languages and confusion can result. In Spanish, *historia* means "history." It also means "story." I recall being amused by a Spanish-speaking patient in a hospital who told me that the doctor was not a good doctor because he didn't believe what his patients told him. "Why do you think he doesn't believe you?" I asked.

The patient told me the doctor was making rounds and approached him, saying, *"¿Y cuál es su historia?"* [And what's your story?] The patient was really upset. He wasn't telling stories! He was telling the truth!

Myth means story. For many it has come to mean a made-up, ridiculous, manipulative falsehood in narrative form, an obvious untruth. The world was *not* made in six days. The globe we are on does *not* have corners, nor does it ride on the backs of four elephants. The moon is *not* made of green cheese. The Creator of the Cosmos was *not* a preying mantis, or a human being. And so forth and so forth.

ે▲

The prevalent and traditional mythology in western culture has been Christianity, and it does try to deal with Death.

"The last enemy to be destroyed is Death."

"Death is swallowed up in victory."

Christianity is a huge and complex tradition, which seems to be waning as a belief-shaping and life-style-governing force. Fewer and fewer people really believe it, fewer and fewer study it, fewer and fewer are able to take it seriously. For many Christianity is infantile and foolish. For them it is a relic of olden days, of childhood, not thought of much, certainly not worked out personally and then affirmed as a belief system.

Two exceptions to those generalizations need to be noted:

[1] Liberation Theology has caught on among the poor and oppressed all over Latin America, and has breathed new life into Christianity, which has traditionally sided with the establishment in that part of the world. It echoes clearly the teachings of Martin Luther King of the black liberation movement in the 60's in the United States. The Pope, and many North Americans, have difficulty with Liberation Theology because of its similarity to, and ties with, revolutionary ideas which can be labeled Marxist, as if Amos and Jesus were Marxists.

[2] Fundamentalism has been a rising tide across the world in all traditions, influencing the lives and belief-systems of a growing number of people. It is authoritarian, telling adherents what they *must* believe. It is allied with and often used by oppressive regimes in different parts of the world. The Fundamentalist Christians are the most active, fastest growing and most politically active segment of Christianity. In our country they have temporarily taken over the Republican Party and the Federal Government. They do not constitute a majority, but behave and talk as if they did.

Fundamentalists in the Vatican elected the last two popes and, along with "contras" funded by the United States government, have virtually stamped out Liberation Theology, leaving misery and poverty and large-scale die-offs in place of any hope for change.

Fundamentalist Muslims have armed themselves and declared war on the United States, and attacked, and sucked our leaders into the no-exit "war on terror."

Fundamentalist Jews insist on not allowing any real peace settlement between Israel and the Palestinians. They believe "God" gave all of Palestine to the Jews.

Many persons in our culture think that "myth" means "lie," because the myths that were presented to them, the old stories that were told, were taken literally by those telling them, and by those hearing them. The fundamentalists take the Biblical myths literally, and thus find themselves in conflict with geologists and biologists and paleontologists.

But the myths were never meant to be taken literally. To do that *is* to believe a lie. But "myth" means "story," and includes not only the stories, but the values behind the stories, and all the implied beliefs about the world and one's self and one's group and about living and dying, that underlie the stories. There is a difference between truth and fact. A story can be true and not fact at all.

If one's myth is still "working," it is something to be lived. A myth is something to *live* by. One aspect of living is its conclusion, and we need to ponder myths to die by. The myths need to be tested, and one of the tests is whether the myth that one is living by will be helpful and *true* in its deepest meaning, as one approaches this final crisis. For instance, if you've been living by the myth that you're special, some kind of exception to all the rules, you'll be caught off guard when the end comes. Or if you think that your myth is that the Creator and Ruler of the Cosmos has a special care for you, but then you live, and approach Death, as if that were not so at all, your myth is false.

Sometimes what's left of an old myth, or old group of myths, is a metaphor. Let's practice this examination by taking a look at the metaphor of The River.

The Bible, John Bunyan's **Pilgrim's Progress**, and several slave spirituals, like "Deep River," all use the metaphor of the river as a boundary, the border of a New Country, a barrier—wide, cold, deep—to be crossed. The river represents Death, and the metaphor says that Death is a transition from one existence to another.

Other myths, originally from further east, use the river as a metaphor for Life. The river is not something you cross. It is a flow you are in, that carries you downstream. It is a flow that you needn't and shouldn't try to push, nor hinder. Indeed, you cannot. The "boundary" at the far end is the ocean, which, in turn, is a symbol of the infinite. It is not a barrier to be overcome, but a vastness, that vastness from which we came and to which we shall return.

For some it seems strange to suggest that we choose among myths and throw out what is erroneous or non-functional. They still have the myths linked to Authority. But we do need to question the ideas and values that underlie the stories. We need to pick and choose, and invent new ones.

When a person carries around, either deliberately or by default, a myth that isn't working, it is a charade, a lie, maybe a mask, maybe a way of deceiving others, most likely a source of self-deception. This is part of what Socrates meant about the unexamined life not being worth living.

We know an elderly lady, ninety-one years old, frail, in pain, nearly blind, contrary as she always was, expecting more attention than her late-middle-aged offspring have time and energy for, which only makes her more angry and more demanding. At one point she began accusing everyone of theft. She claimed jewelry was missing and accused one of her sons of taking it. A daughter found the jewelry and tried to mollify her and get her attention away from the idea of theft. "You don't need to be worrying about that jewelry anymore anyway. You need to tend to your soul. You and God—"

The old lady interrupted. "I don't believe there *is* a God." The statement was so flat that it stopped the conversation.

She attended church all her life. Many, but not all, of her offspring are church people. What is this? For eighty-some years she accepted that myth, only to blow it all away at the end in disbelief. And now she lacks a belief system which could perhaps help her to be gracious and gentle and thoughtful and courageous in the last days.

Taking a half-baked version of the Christian myth literally, without thinking about it, can pre-empt time and opportunity better spent wondering and asking questions and sharing doubts with other people. Heaven, hell, St. Peter, pearly gates, cloud-riding, free harp lessons—those symbols are worn out, and they are really not useful. It would be more helpful to ponder life-cycles, processes, the flow, giving and receiving, the roundness and the eternal return.

We need to do some fresh thinking, now while we have our wits and some energy and some room to maneuver. If we come up with some myths that we think we could die by, we'll have to *live* by them, too, and that'll involve changing some things, most likely. We need to do this, if we're going to, before emphysema and Alzheimer's syndrome stop us. On the deathbed is too late.

All Christian deathbed repentance stories detract from this enterprise. If a person spends his life doing bad things, and then says he's sorry at the end, very little of substance is changed. If that kind of myth-to-die-by enables some scoundrel to squeeze through that gate, my view is that the selfish, thoughtless, ego-centered person *did not change.* This is the myth of Don Juan, told in stories and plays and operas, and is unworthy of serious consideration. A lying, murdering destroyer of other persons' lives remains what he always was to the end. It's no way to live, and unconvincing as a trick to die by.

I suspect my father had the opposite problem. He was too hard on himself. I think he found himself believing only part of his myth. He didn't believe the part about grace and love and forgiveness, but was left believing in punishment. He might have had an easier time of it, if he could have lost his "faith" entirely.

We humans tell each other stories which reinforce our values and our belief-systems. I'm wondering about myths to die by. "Name or describe briefly a myth, which, when believed, enables a person to die in peace."

I tried that on a poet friend and she ducked, or so I thought. She didn't name a myth at all. "A.A. has the answer to that," she said. She was referring to Alcoholics Anonymous. "You leave it in the hands of a Higher Power."

I was struck with a strong sense of irony. I had just finished an early draft of a book, which I was then calling, **God Anonymous**. The basic idea, taken from A.A., suggested that "God" may be the very obsession people need to get over, or be cured of, or bring under control at least. "On Finding Relief from an Obsession," was the subtitle. When the book was finally published, it was called, **Freedom from God: Restoring the Sense of Wonder**.

All that bounced in my head as my poet friend and I studied each other. Higher Power? Which one? Gravitation? Entropy? No, she means God. Which God?

"What if you don't believe in any such Higher Power?" I asked her. "What if there *is* no Higher Power?" But there is. There's Gravitation, and Entropy, if nothing else.

"Animals go into shock and die in peace," she told me. "Traumatized humans have the sense of 'giving in' at the end."

She's right about that part. I experienced that exact sensation fifty years ago in a flash in the middle of a car wreck. "Oh! O.K., if that's how it has to be—!" I was ready to go gentle, and others have reported to me similar experiences.

My poet friend and I did not settle it. She seemed to be concluding that one had to believe in something, but I was left with the need to continue to ponder it.

I have pondered a great deal. I gathered as many as I could of the images, the metaphors, the beliefs that people hold or claim to hold that have to do with the fact that we die. I have not hesitated to evaluate these metaphors and beliefs. They can be classified according to their sources. Some come from infantile wishing. Some come from the contemporary media and others from socio-political movements. These myths function by default, if persons haven't thought about these matters much.

Many widely-held beliefs are left over from religious loyalty. These stories and metaphors are similar in that they enhance ego, that is, they help believers preserve the concept of ego, their own ego, intact, in one way or another.

I have arranged these beliefs and stories in what I have come to regard as roughly ascending order of usefulness to thoughtful mortals. Someone else may want to arrange them differently. Practical observation has supplied several myths, and they may be very helpful, especially since they are based on truth rather than someone's power play, or wishing. Neither wishing nor power makes something so that isn't so.

The last category, and possibly most helpful, is entitled, "Stories from Philosophy, which Transcend Ego." This is practical observation with a difference. On the assumption that the ego is a necessary fiction, but fiction nonetheless, what can we believe, or train ourselves to practice thinking, that will help us confront that pending dissolution?

I find it very exhilarating to talk about this and share uncertainties. I find my sense of wonder growing and expanding. We are very mysterious beings in the midst of a great mystery.

ያ▲ያ▲ያ▲

V

STORIES FROM INFANTILE WISHING

For cynics, as we have noted already, the word "myth" is a synonym for "lie." Some question whether it's a good idea to expose children to myths at all, since they'll only have to outgrow them and get used to the truth, later. I must admit that I felt that way about Santa Claus at one time. I still have some difficulty with that myth, mainly with those parents who insist to their little children that there *really is* a Santa Claus, and then jump all over those of us who are "straightening them out," whether deliberately or inadvertently.

I remember my mother saying to me when I was seven and my sisters were two and three, "*You* understand about Santa Claus. It's make-believe. But let's *do* make believe, for Ann and Sue. It's not true, but we'll just go ahead and pretend it is. O.K.?" I don't remember *ever* believing it was true, that is, literally true. But we all enjoyed the fat little guy and the reindeer.

Parents who make a big deal out of Santa Claus are doing to this myth what the literalists do to the Bible. They make it preposterous, and strain the child's ability to trust the parents' word, since they are insisting on something which the child can finally no longer believe—all that nonsense about the North Pole and toys for everyone and a flying sleigh.

But if everyone knows it's a myth, we can all make believe together, and there's little harm done. Rampant commercialism has almost completely spoiled this particular myth anyway, and literalism is not a huge problem here.

A myth is a belief, with accompanying and supporting

stories. Rudolph, the reindeer with the glowing nose, has been added to the Santa Claus myth during the adult memory of many of us—a new detail, a new little story which builds on the older framework. How many kids believe it's really true? How many adults want the kids to believe it? We're just pretending, aren't we? It's make-believe, isn't it?

But what does Santa Claus have to do with real life? Not much, one could say at first glance, but if you keep looking at it, you're not so sure. Retail sales in capitalist countries depend a great deal, some would say too much, on the myth of Santa Claus. If widespread disbelief in "Christmas" set in, the economy would be in more trouble than it already is.

One of the greatest threats to stability to come out of the Vietnam War protest movement was the suggestion that we suspend all celebration of Christmas until the slaughter was stopped. The authorities stopped it at about the same time the plan was offered, so this suggestion was never fully tested.

I think it would have been harder to stop Christmas than it was to stop the war, because Christmas involves two competing mythologies: family good feeling, generosity, giving and sharing on the one hand, and buying and buying to impress people on the other hand.

The war had only one myth behind it: macho strutting and pretending to be tough, while real people who had no reason to be angry with one another killed and maimed each other. It was remarkable how it did stop finally. We simply quit doing it, which is what the protestors said all along had to be done, and machismo has never fully recovered, Rambo to the contrary notwithstanding. We can all be thankful. When the lessons of Vietnam are finally fully digested, we'll all understand better what's been going on lately in the Middle East.

The Santa Claus story itself admittedly doesn't have much to do directly with dying. It is used here to illustrate infantilism. Infantilism as a state of mind is totally self-centered and quite unrealistic, as are the beliefs, stories and metaphors derived from it. Some of our beliefs and ideas about death can correctly be labeled "infantile."

A. It Can't Happen Here

This assertion is patently absurd on its surface, yet it enjoys wide popularity. "It can't happen to us." Stock market crashes, imperial collapses, successful revolutions, total runaway inflation—the kinds of developments that make history interesting, or boring, depending on how it's taught—these things always happen somewhere else, we think. World leaders and world taxpayers and world voters insist on paying no attention to what has already happened, and persist in believing that what took place in ancient Rome, or in China once upon a time, or in the USA in 1929, cannot happen "here."

"It can't happen to me." We spend a good bit of our time living as if we were not going to die. William Saroyan reportedly was taken completely by surprise during the last half hour of his life. "I thought I was an exception!" he exclaimed.

On my way home from my father's emphysema funeral I studied carefully the faces of intelligent-looking people, as they smoked in airport waiting areas. "Self-destruction is powerful stuff," I noted in my journal.

Letters we read together in the attic the day of my mother's funeral reveal that my father kept his younger brother in tobacco, when they were both teenagers. When my father was twenty-two, finding money for tobacco was still a major concern. There is no doubt in my mind that tobacco shortened my father's life. He could have lived to be a hundred, like his grandmother, but for lack of air. He didn't think, as a teenager, and like many a teenager today, that it could happen to him.

I've met smokers who say, "I'm going to die anyway. Why should you object, if I want to kill myself smoking?" It's a courageous-sounding tack, but I suspect there is more bluster than courage in it, and the bluster is aided by the myth which says, "I'm an exception." This cynical view of life strikes me as sad, if it is sincere. It pretends to say, "My life is over anyway, so what do you care, and why should I care?" My selfish objection to the smoking is that the statistics concerning these suicidal persons are included with those of us non-smokers in the tables used by most medical insurance companies.

George Burns, cigar and all, found remarkable comic material in his energetic old age. The joke was that maybe he wouldn't die. "Dying's an over-rated act. It's been done before." He was right in playing it that way. Not-dying has never been played before. The question was, "Can he pull it off?" While we chuckled at his comedy routine, and admired his courage and his energy, we didn't believe it. And finally, we were proven right, once again.

"It can't happen to me," seems silly, when taken literally regarding one's own life span. One can resolve to take care of oneself, and perhaps live longer. My own unscientifically arrived-at formula is to be busy with interesting tasks and projects, and let Death interrupt. But to pretend that, in one's own case, Death isn't going to interrupt ever, is to slip into megalomania and unreality.

Perhaps you heard of the fellow who jumped out of the Empire State Building. As he passed the thirty-ninth floor, he was heard to yell, "So far, so good!"

That reminds me of another old fellow who was asked, "Are you immortal?"

He answered, "So far!" Maybe he knew what he was doing, but it seems more likely that he thought he was an exception. "I'm special. It can't happen to me. That kind of thing happens to other people only. I don't need to follow instructions. The rules are for the others." It's preposterous.

Life has a way of pulling us all into line, especially near the end. John White, in his book, **A Practical Guide to Death and Dying**, notes how the fear of death can be broken down:

[1] fear of pain
[2] fear of loss
[3] fear of the unknown
[4] fear of meaninglessness
[5] fear of non-being

He takes us into deep mythological questions. Man is mortal. What is, or ought to be, immortal? Surely not the body. It does finally wear out. The pattern does not hold. In Gulliver's third voyage he visits the Struldbrugs. They were people who were immortal. That is, they didn't die. But they continued to age. They became weaker, and sicker and thinner and feebler and more and more miserable, and never died. Gulliver reported that after visiting them his "lust for immortality was much abated."

I recall the daughter who told her aged and feeble mother that she needn't be worrying about whether anyone did or did not steal her jewelry—"You need to be looking out for your *soul!*"

What is *soul*? The Greek word translated "soul" is "Psyche," and means Mind, or Life. "You need to be looking out for your *life!*" Your very inner Life. That which survives, if anything does. Whether anything survives or not, we need a word for it, if we're to talk about it.

Your Self. Eastern myths speak of the Self of the World. "God" is not an exact translation. The Self. THE SELF. IT. THAT which expresses ITSELF through you, and me, and everyone. In those Eastern cultures that little bow, with the hands clasped in front, upon meeting someone, even a stranger on the road, acknowledges that SELF in the other. "You need to be looking after your SELF!" meaning that deep inner core in there, which is so deep it's beyond "selfishness."

One is not always so sure of himself or herself to be able to say flatly, "Why, certainly, human personalities, or souls, or something, survive death. The universe can't afford to throw away something that valuable." One isn't quite sure enough of one's own value to be able to assert that, about oneself.

But, looking outward—seeing you, my precious, knowing you, taking you into account, enables me to assert, quite sure of myself, "Why, certainly, human personalities, or souls, or something, survive death. The universe can't afford to throw away something that valuable!"

And maybe that's no more than a statement of how valuable someone is to me. Maybe it's just an expression of need, from my end. Maybe it doesn't *prove* anything. But it feels that it ought to. Tchaikovsky is accused of being sentimental in his music, even self-pitying. Maybe so. In any case he and his music come to mind at this moment. I know that, for me, his Sixth Symphony is a statement similar to the one I made just above, about souls surviving. "Maybe it all merely comes to an end. If so, I think it should not. Beauty, life, joy and truth persist, or should, if they don't. Where did my sense of the worth of such things come from? This music reminds me of how beautiful it all is. Here is how precious it is. Not me, It. THAT." One thing I know for certain: when I get out of myself, and more into THAT, I feel more alive.

Having said that much about the desired survival of the soul, or something, whatever we're to call it, we have inched a step beyond merely stating that Death is something that only others are going to have to experience. Surely, that's progress, on beyond infantilism.

B. It's All Mine

Another preposterous and dangerous belief to live by is, "It's all mine." Corollaries include, "I am superior. I am owner. I am master. I am in no way obligated to anyone for anything. It is all mine." So I can take it, if I want to, and use it all up, kill every last one, befoul, subdivide, sell, poison, or destroy—anything and everything.

This myth would be too utterly preposterous to take

seriously, except for the fact that large numbers of us are living exactly that way. The environmental movement is pleading, rather gently I would say, for sanity, but the illogic steamrolls on. "You can't stop progress."

It doesn't seem to do any good to remind people that with no environment, there will be no economy of any kind, that with nuclear winter, there will be no paying jobs nor fringe benefits, that when the oxygen, ozone, fresh water and plankton, or any one of them, are gone, we'll be gone. Usually people reply by saying, "Well, if we're all gone, it won't matter." I have never understood that answer. It seems to be saying, "If we kill ourselves, it's all right." I for one think it is not.

Many stories are told, but they seem to do no good in dissuading this insane culture from its own self-destruction. And not just our culture. A Guatemalan lady told me, "You exterminated your Indians, and now we're exterminating ours." A Brazilian told me, "You cut down your forests, and now we're cutting down ours." Read **Collapse**, by Jared Diamond.

In my feverish imagination I came up with a useful function for the Pentagon. Secure the agreement and full assistance of NATO, Russia and China, and then together invade the rain forest, erect a chain-link fence around it, and annihilate anyone who tries to enter. Also execute summarily anyone who lays a sharp instrument of any kind up against a tree… But it won't happen. It isn't even a good idea. It's just an overblown fantasy, another expression, in fact, in reverse maybe, of the myth which says, "It's all mine, so my violence is justified."

We're looking at the beliefs and metaphors we use that come from our infancy. The nursing child lives in a very small world, and he thinks it's all his. His crib, his body, his mother's breast, her face—it is all his. Growing up, for some, consists in arranging things so that the same enlarged infant owns and controls, by force and by crying tantrums, his whole world. Such a person tends not to be interested much in geography and politics, let alone astronomy and galaxies, because of the strain such outside information will put on the belief system he's using.

"It's all mine," is a motto by which ego-centered people deny death altogether. To say it is unrealistic understates the matter badly. The quest for "security," by which financial security is usually meant, is an expression of this vain hope. In the real world dying and living are really very similar. In each case we have to let the next thing happen. We have to let go. We cannot be assured of "success" in life, and there is no security, either in life or death.

Many people define both Success and Security in terms of this "it's all mine" myth. They want their acquisitiveness and their sense of possession to be guaranteed, all the way to the end and past the end. They want their temporary sense of ownership to outlast and transcend the very cycles of life. But life is meant to be *lived*, not spent or wasted, trying to guarantee Success. It is foolish to squander all one's energy and time on Security, when there is none.

"Ships are safe in harbor, but that is not what ships are for."

"*Here we have no lasting city.*"

"You die, anyway."

C. The Dog in the Manger

One of Aesop's fables describes how some people live, and then die. It is a sort of corollary to the idea of ownership discussed in the previous section.

The dog in the manger couldn't eat the hay there, but he wouldn't let the burro eat it either. Some humans have taken that same attitude toward their own lives. "I can't enjoy mine, for whatever reason—pain, shame, rejection, weakness, decrepitude—so I'm going to make sure you don't enjoy yours either." These are the most unpopular sick-a-bed patients, but they also can be unpleasant spouses, or parents, or children. "My life is unhappy, and I'm going to make sure yours is, too." Misery loves company, as we've all heard.

The Roman Emperor Tiberius provided an extreme case of this. He gave orders, in advance, that on the occasion of his death, a large number of army personnel of all ranks were to be killed, in order to guarantee that there be universal mourning when it happened. Otherwise, there would have been very little mourning, and considerable celebration, since he was such an evil and bloody scoundrel.

Some contemporary world leaders have had this same view. Their principle motive is their own aggrandizement, and they show little evidence of caring whether or not the species survives the current crises, whether the life process continues on our ailing planet, or whether the world goes on spinning, after they are gone.

At the bottom of it, in the case of Tiberius and his modern counterparts, we find necrophilia, "love of Death," an abhorrence of Life, and a very cavalier attitude toward life-forms generally. Do we really need twenty thousand and more nuclear warheads to be "modernized" at great expense? We are puzzled about what to do with the lethal waste which their production leaves lying around. And besides, a few dozen such warheads will suffice to annihilate us all. Do we really need *more* nerve gas? Who will write the history book in which the Memorial End of the World is named for President Whatsisname?

"I'll take a lot of 'em with me, when I go." It's a line from the cheap movies of decades ago, and it is infantile behavior.

We'll look further at necrophilia later. Here, looking at the Dog in the Manger, is the place to discuss deathbed promises. This is the moment when the one dying seeks to extend his power and influence beyond the reach of his own lifetime. We've all watched it, or heard of it, and seen people regulating their lives decades later on the basis of promises made at a deathbed. I believe it is immoral to extract such a promise, and it is infantile and foolish to consent to one. If you did make such a promise, and are letting it govern your life, you may release yourself now. You were acting under duress—someone was dying!—and you temporarily let go of the responsibility for running your own life. You may take back that responsibility, now.

My father tried to extract a deathbed promise from me, that I should "move back to Pennsylvania, soon and permanently." But I didn't take the bait, and the open revelation of his final power play amounted to the final release for me. "Nothing will please him, short of abject obedience," I said to myself, and stood firm.

It was the old dog-in-the-manger ploy, on his part. "I'm dying. I'll be gone. But I'll still be running things. I'll still have it all *my way*. I'll still be making you and them all miserable."

Don't do this. Don't ask it, if you're the one dying. And don't allow it, if you're the one being asked. Just laugh it off, and say, "No promises."

If each one of us is busy living his or her own life to the full, with no manipulation of the other people around, but rather loving and thoughtful cooperation, this won't come up. Deathbed promises come up when something is unresolved and untended to. So, tend to it, in advance, if you possibly can.

Some people play games with a strategy that includes hindering the opponent. In baseball and football it's called "defense," and is a legitimate half of the process. But in other games, like Chinese checkers, it amounts to a delay in getting one's own task finished, and hinders winning.

My father played games that way. He'd hurt his own game in order to obstruct his opponent. From this perspective I believe it was a clue to his life. He was essentially ego-centered. His game-playing and his rules for kids-raising proved it. And then when it came time to give up ego altogether, that is *die*, he was terrified, and resisted, and dragged others down with him.

Ego is the problem. Childhood is the time for strengthening ego, so that one can become an active self-propelled, self-reliant, productive adult. But the second half of life requires that we put ego back in its place. It is a project worthy of considerable attention and energy.

Now is the time to go to work on it, so that ego does not outlast one's resolve to be fully alive, while one *is* alive. Live to the full, paying close attention, remembering, imagining, making order out of confusion, listening, discerning, allowing, harnessing and making the most of whatever comes along. Live and give to the full—and then be done and gone with a smile.

D. Someday My Prince Will Come

Another attitude which ultimately fails as a sustaining idea to live and then die by is, "Someday my prince will come." We all know the fairy tale to which Walt Disney added this song. Snow White is safe with the dwarves, but trapped at the same time. There she sits, waiting to be rescued. Someone else, some rescuer, will have to come, and she's trusting that he will indeed someday come. Waiting and depending on a Savior is an infantile way of handling life, and Death.

There are many variations on this same theme. "You do it for me." My father had a dozen or more people praying that he would die. It was something they had to do, he thought, not he.

"I'll meet the right guy, or gal, someday." This is waiting, vegetating meanwhile maybe, not actively doing or being. This is depending on some outside force, some agency other than oneself.

"Messiah will come." This entails the belief that history itself is in the hands of a Divine Being, who will tend to things when he's good and ready. It's a doctrine which thrives among the oppressed victims of historical forces of various kinds—slavery, discrimination, genocide. It may be a survival mechanism, but it is not a doctrine which changes things much.

It must be said that in two remarkable cases the belief in a Divine-Saving-Agent-to-Come contributed in an important way to the continuation of the victimized group which held that belief. I'm thinking first of the Jews in Europe over the centuries of persecution at the hands of the Christians, during which time the Jews resisted remarkably little, but instead leaned on this faith in the coming of the Messiah. They survived, even though Messiah hasn't come yet. The emphasis among most Jews generally seems to have shifted recently, but this belief in the coming Messiah must get some of the credit for the fact that they preserved their group identity in spite of all the genocide they have suffered.

Likewise, the black slaves in North America developed a remarkable religion of patient dependence on divine power, not relying on human resistance or human aid, and they did outlast the institution of slavery. Whenever they fought, their Christian masters were ready to exterminate them and did, but this passive faith helped preserve them in spite of that.

Having said that, I go back to my original observation, that the myth of a rescuer may not be the best kind of help for most of us in getting through life. Joseph Campbell describes the life of Everyman as the journey of the hero, in his remarkable book, **Hero with a Thousand Faces**. One section is entitled, "The Call to Adventure." This is the knock of opportunity, the unexpected opening in the hedge that hems in our life. It is the beginning of the journey.

The next section is entitled, "Refusal of the Call." The opening words are important:

> Often in actual life, and not infrequently in the myths and popular tales, we encounter the dull case of the call unanswered, for it is always possible to turn the ear to other interests. Refusal of the summons converts the adventure into its negative. Walled in boredom, hard work, or "culture," the subject loses the power of significant affirmative action and becomes a victim to be saved.

Instead of becoming the hero, one turns into the kind of victim some other hero may or may not come rescue.

"Someday My Prince Will Come." The variation for the male victims awaiting rescue, would be, "Someday My Princess Will Come." In many cases one may read "Mom," in place of "Princess." People allow a great deal of life to get away, sometimes, before coming to grips with the task of declaring independence from Mother and embarking on a life of their own.

There are additional variations on the same theme: "Daddy will come fix it." Or, "My old man can lick your old man." They are infantile on the surface, but many live according to some version of those notions.

"Science will discover something to solve that problem." "Technology will get us out of this predicament." I know people who believe that overpopulation is not and never will be a real problem, because science and technology will come up with solutions before we have to bother with unpleasantness or hard decisions. But we are already in trouble. Famine confronts many already, and grinding poverty. Technology already is offering genetic tampering, death ray weapons, cybernetic control of society and our private lives, nuclear winter and nuclear waste—what science is coming up with frankly doesn't look like a solution to me. And all of that is the tip of a huge iceberg, the small non-secret, publicly acknowledged fraction of a huge batch of not-quite-imaginable pending problems.

"The Doctor will fix it." My father believed that to the bitter end. During his last days, I found myself feeling glad that I had fought off his earlier pressures that I become a doctor. That would have caused him even more disappointment. "Can the doctor keep you from dying? You die anyway."

My friend's grandmother lived a full life all her life with no sourness, no bitterness, and she refused to be frightened into surgery at age ninety-eight. "You'll die, if you don't!" the doctors warned her.

"I'll die anyway, eventually," she retorted, and has passed the century mark and is still going strong. She's not claiming to be able to escape death. But she's not in thrall to the medical establishment either. Some of the claims of that establishment verge on blackmail, and so do the charges for their services. "How much is your mother's life worth? Well, then, pay here." And you owe it, even if they *don't* save the life of your loved one who was threatened. They want us to believe they *can* fix it. And they want us to pay, a-plenty, whether they do or whether they don't.

The scientists have become the new priests. Even the TV ads depend upon them to mousetrap what's left of our capacity for logical thinking, persuading us to believe those actors in white coats. This pill will do this. This drug will do that. Nine million doctors can't be wrong. Let Daddy fix it. I, for one, do not believe that Daddy will come fix it.

The old priesthood still wields power, too. The concepts of Savior and Salvation are basic to Christianity, and distinguish it notably from the other major religions of mankind. The message is that humanity is hopelessly wicked and lost, doomed to be condemned by Divine Justice. But the Savior has overridden the badness, and divine fiat has approved, salvaging some individuals from the pending conflagration. The species, and the planet, will be burned. Salvation consists in being removed from this burning mess and taken away to a safe place to be with the Savior.

These are mythological images, not really taken very seriously anymore by most thoughtful people—yet the implications as to our actual situation, our condition, our responsibility and our duty to change things are very serious. It is infantile to believe that we only have to be concerned about our own personal "safety." Yet this childishness has reached into high places in the political structure.

I was dumfounded when I learned that a former Secretary of the Interior, to be left nameless here and hopefully forgotten sooner, did not believe we needed an Environmental Protection

Agency, even though Congress had made it part of his department. The environment doesn't need protecting, he said, because Jesus is coming to take the believers to heaven and the rest will go to hell and there won't even *be* an environment after that. And he believed it would happen soon, while he was still in office.

I think it is foolish that we allow such myths to hold sway in such high places. A President who believes in Armageddon is a threat to the Biosphere itself, given the weapons of mass destruction which he has available, both nuclear and biological. "God will take care of things," they say. I'm sorry, but I think we'd better take care of things ourselves, if there's still time.

E. Going Home

In many old songs and stories dying is referred to as crossing over a barrier, a river, for instance. The river is variously described as cold, wide and deep, as if to suggest that the crossing is not easy.

All these myths suggest that something awaits the traveler on the other side, that Death is not Blotto, but transition.

We must pause here and admit that we are not in an area where we have scientific or legal proof. We are in an area of belief, of faith. Maybe we are in the presence of plain old wishful thinking. If we are, we ought to be honest about it.

Is there Another Side? Does there need to be? Bernie, while dying, while no longer able to communicate with us because cancer had damaged her brain, called out across that great gulf, "Hello! Hello—hello!" It was thought-provoking to watch. She never gave a clue as to what she saw or expected, and maybe she was only acting out universal habits of wishful thinking.

I have never received a communication from the other side. And I *have* listened. Sitting here writing all this material opens me up and would provide a very good occasion for someone to communicate with me: Jeannie, who died of leukemia at age sixteen writing poems about perfection; Mr. Mitman, who taught me farming; Alice and Martha, who gave and gave all their lives without receiving much in return that one could notice; Bob Stetler, my high school classmate and the first to go; Uncle Jack, Uncle Tom, Uncle Sandy, Uncle Allen, Grandmother Great, Aunt Mary, Mom, Dad—no one has made a peep.

The fact that so many other-side stories tell of going home makes me suspicious that it may well be an infantile notion. "I wanta go home," meaning back to the home of my childhood, back to the Auld Country. Many elderly people feel this urge in a kind of geographical sense. Some birds and some fish do it, in spite of formidable obstacles. Lassie went home. Salmon try to. Maybe it's in our physical nature, this yearning to go back to the childhood home.

I don't feel much of it. The area I came from is beautiful at certain times of year, but I don't want to live there. I was too unhappy while there, too oppressed. I am enjoying freedom and responsibility too much to want to go back to the scene of dependency and submission.

I had visited my parents briefly the summer before they died. As I was leaving, my father said, "We may never see each other again."

"That's true," I replied.

"If it's to happen, it'll have to be in heaven," he said.

"Yes, perhaps," I said.

"I hope so," he persisted. *He* was not at all sure that *I* was going to heaven.

"I hope so, too," I said. But it was a lie. How could both of us go to heaven and it still *be* heaven? If he can continue to lord it over me, it won't be heaven for me. It'll fit perfectly the definition of hell! I've been there already! But if he can't lord it over me anymore, it won't be heaven for him. For us to be together and it be heaven for both, he'd have to adapt to a changed relationship, and he spent all his life *not* adapting.

Changing, allowing change, wanting change and affirming change—that'll feel like hell to him!

So, if dying means going home to deceased elderly loved ones, that puts me off. I do not want, anymore, to have to fend off that authority. It is a dilemma.

Maybe for those who found family life as children a happy time, dying can be thought of comfortably as going home. I find very few such people, however, not counting those whose testimony about their childhood I simply do not believe.

"Home is when you go there, they have to take you in," wrote Robert Frost. Maybe that's it. Acceptance of some kind awaits us on the other side. Even if we're buried in unconsecrated ground, and condemned on *this* side, we're going home.

Some have never known a home, and long for one. Some have had homes they'd have been better off without. Whatever awaits us, it has to be fair for everybody—so it could be this isn't going to be the best universal metaphor. You can tell I'm having my problems with it.

There are all kinds of homes, for that matter. I do not want to return to my childhood home, which was essentially, from my point of view, an unjust situation. The home I am in now is good for me—there is fairness and equality and affection and good humor and compassion. I don't need to die in order to "go home." I *am* home. I belong here. I'm not certain about what's "over there."

Those who are sure about what's on the other side seem to have some kind of advantage, as we all confront Death. I don't know how they became so certain. When they try to share their certainty with me, I am mostly impressed by their arrogance, and find myself turned off.

ào

F. Going to Heaven

The myth we learned as children stated that when we died, we'd go to heaven. Heaven was in the sky, above the clouds. Later we learned that in other languages "heaven" and "sky" were both indicated by the same word—for instance, *cielo* in Spanish. In that language the words of our myth meant, "When we die, we'll go to the sky." I must say it seemed a little farfetched, even then.

"The Heavenly Father" was the same as the Celestial Father, which was the same as the Sky-Father. Then along come all the myths of all the world, which describe the Sky-Father as the male patriarchal consort of the Earth-Mother. There was no Earth-Mother in the Reformation Christianity of my childhood, although we heard about the Virgin Mother Mary from Roman Catholic neighbors. The notion of dying and going to Heaven emphasized going to be with the Sky/Father.

An Old Testament story tells how the prophet Elijah was separated from his successor, Elisha, shortly after they crossed the Jordan River, by a chariot of fire and horses of fire. And then it says, "Elijah went up by a whirlwind into heaven." That is, into the sky. The old spiritual song, "Swing Low, Sweet Chariot," suggests that Elijah and others later went up *in* the chariot, but the text of the story doesn't say that.

Jesus "ascended into heaven," i.e., into the sky, according to the New Testament and the Apostles' Creed. The New Testament doesn't say true believers are going to follow him there, but rather that he's to return from there in the same way, descending, I suppose, as the clouds separate.

We don't need to belabor this anymore. The old myth is not to be taken literally. We know that we are not living in a three-story universe, with Heaven above and Hell beneath, with a flat Earth in the middle. Therefore Heaven/Sky is not a *place* where Elijah and Jesus and True Believers go. At best it is a direction. Not "up there," but "out there." But even that doesn't help us much. Are we to suppose that the Heavenly Father is in Outer Space, and that Jesus and the rest will go to meet him there? Where? Is it a place at all? Can it be?

"It's a mystery," authority will say. Yes, it sure is, but if that means we're supposed to quit thinking about it, I refuse to do that.

Literal bodily survival on some planet not yet discovered makes no sense to me. Rejection of this myth is easy, almost too easy. You heard of the astronaut who *did* stumble on Heaven in his celestial journeys, and was giving a news conference on his return. The reporters were agog. "You saw God? You met with God?"

"Yep. Sure did."

"Well, tell us, what is God like?"

"Well, to begin with, she's black."

That's an oldie, by now, supposed to help get rid of the old white male red-blooded American war god, who spells his name, G-O-D. It hasn't yet gotten rid of him, however.

Another more recent version concludes with the line, "Yes, I met God. And is she ever angry!" But these stories aren't really helping us much.

Someone tried to comfort me after the last funeral at which I officiated. Or maybe they simply wanted said out loud what I *didn't* say in the formal service. "Now Jeannie's with Jesus in heaven."

I had studied too much astronomy. I'd watched leukemia destroy her bit by bit for too long. Where is she? Some of her is in this box. What part of her is elsewhere? How so? Where? I didn't believe enough of it anymore; the words were too glib and the attitude too smug.

Yet some of her is alive in my mind, in my memory even after almost forty years. An aspect of her continues. I haven't spent much energy imagining what sort of woman she'd have become, what sort of companion and mother. She's frozen at age

sixteen in my memory. Besides, that's *me*, not her. Where is *she*?
I don't know. Her last poems spoke of perfection, and I still
wonder what she meant. To tell me that she's in the sky is little
comfort.

꽃꽃꽃

VI

STORIES FROM CONTEMPORARY MEDIA

The media has replaced the home as the shaper of the attitudes, the values, the beliefs, and very thoughts with which we think. No one is totally beyond that influence. The strictest possible critique of the media will still be permeated with ideas and images and turns of phrase that have come from that very same media.

"Death is unAmerican, and an affront to every citizen's right to life, liberty and the pursuit of happiness," wrote Arnold Toynbee, the British historian. He didn't think our American culture dealt very well with death.

The Hemlock Society made a similar observation in one of their brochures. "Dying is regarded as bad taste in this society, despite the fact that ten out of ten people do it."

Much of what we believe about death comes from the contemporary media. If we decide, after careful consideration, that some of the myths and metaphors from the media are foolish, or even dangerous, that doesn't mean they aren't important. The media itself, being the source and vehicle of these myths, makes them powerful. The default factor, which works in the cases of those who prefer not to think about any of this at all, makes them doubly powerful.

 है

A. I Can Make It Alone

We Americans are famous for our commitment to individualism. In the sense of uplifting and enhancing the worth of each particular human being, the attitude may be called a good thing. When individualism comes into conflict with the good of the group, the results are not always so fine.

We have heard the arguments: "I worked hard and made my fortune; why should I give it away so others don't have to work?"

"Everybody has to figure life out for himself and make the best he can of it."

"There are casualties in any struggle; the superior ones are the ones that make it to the top."

"It's not a concern of mine, if others choose to play when there's work to be done."

"Am I my brother's keeper?"

One of our folk heroes is Daniel Boone, the "pioneer," who kept moving further into the "wilderness," because he couldn't stand neighbors. He meant white folks. The land he was moving into was teeming with people that he didn't think counted, because they were the original occupants of the land he was trespassing on and planning to steal. Not counting them, he seemed to be searching for loneliness.

A line in Sartre's **No Exit** tells what followers of this myth really think. The play is a conversation, taking place in hell. One of the participants states, "Hell is other people."

Solitude is very fine, and some of it from time to time is even necessary. However, nothing but solitude forever and ever is part of the old image of hell, used by both Dante and C. S. Lewis. Isolation, total lack of communication, exile, loneliness —that's the hell most of us think of and dread. But there are extreme individualists who think that hell is other people.

We are born into a human group. Our identity comes from

the group. We learn our language from the group, and use the group's language all our lives. We learn what to do with life itself from the group. Growing up consists of becoming partially distinct from the original group, which we call family, or tribe. But powerful forces drive us on to form new family groups, of one kind or another. The notion that there is such a thing as a "self-made man," or woman, who has not received anything from anyone and who doesn't need anyone, is contrary to the facts of human growth. Nevertheless that notion lies at the bottom of many a story now being told in the contemporary media.

Humans are social beings. I recall standing with my wife and another couple in a long cafeteria line which curved back on itself, so that we were facing the people behind us in line. As we moved, we "met" a continuing parade of people, up quite close. It was more intense than sitting on a bench in the shopping mall and watching all the strange and beautiful people going by. I commented quietly to my companion, "Aren't people marvelous?"

He stunned us all, including some of those passing in front of us, with a loud bark, "I hate people!" We never quite got over it. Deep friendship never developed between the couples—after all, we're people, too, and feel uncomfortable in the presence of hatred. The couple was later divorced. The man was giving this individualism myth a good try, thinking he could make it alone, but we were never sure that he was doing very well.

Sometimes the impermanence of our human relationships hurts so badly that survivors become cautious, fearful of forming new connections, which will only be broken later. I'm not sure what caused my cafeteria-line "friend" to hate people so, but it may well have been some previous loss. One man told me he'd never have a dog again, because they die on you, and the pain was too much. Another older, more bitter man regretted having had children, he said, because "they only grow up and go away and forget you and lead lives of their own, and even *die!*"—he was wishing he had felt less and given less, which seemed a little like wishing he hadn't lived at all.

Grief, when someone dies, or when a relationship dies, is a mixture of things—guilt, regret, loss, the feeling of abandonment. Those feelings can come, even if there is no dead body to grieve over. A numbness, a deadness, the zombie-feeling, which is more like no feeling at all—that can happen when you lose a lover or a friend, when you have to give up on a relationship, for one reason or another. I felt it with my parents, years before they died, when they wouldn't allow an adult relationship.

At such times, this myth is tempting. "I can make it by myself." "Who cares?" "Who needs people?" It is a fake, however, an over-reaction, a period of one's life one has to get through, adapting to the loss of that particular relationship. But a life with *no* relationships, no caring, no commitment, no other people to share life with, is a permanent zombie state.

The media can't push this myth too far, because businesses need customers. Leaders need followers. Speakers need hearers. Writers need readers, sooner or later. Almost everyone needs and welcomes a helper, a companion, a friend.

Bumper stickers are a source of wisdom, sometimes, or at least clues to what others think. "The more I learn about men, the better I like my dog." And the retort: "The more I learn about women, the better I like my truck." These assertions are not particularly flattering to humans, but they nevertheless reveal that the authors are not pretending to be able to make it quite totally alone.

A woman explained to me why she bought a toy poodle. "They love people." Her husband was bed-ridden with cancer. "But the dog doesn't care. He jumps up on the bed to lick and be hugged. The smell doesn't bother him, like it does our human visitors. He just gives love, and my husband needs it. We both need it." We are not alone in this world, not as alone as it feels at the worst of times. We weren't designed to be alone, the good myths all say.

But old songs and spirituals suggest that dying is necessarily a lonely matter.

> You must make your lonesome journey.
> You must make it by yourself.
> Oh, nobody else can make it for you.
> You have to make it by yourself.

When I ask people, "And what don't you like about dying?" the same answer comes often: "Each one has to do it alone."

A younger couple startled us the other day by announcing that they had made a suicide agreement. When either one of them is in the condition that they see their own parents in right now, they will together take themselves off the scene. They did not appear to be kidding us or each other. I was touched by their devotion to each other, and their rejection of the future roles of invalid, or survivor, for either one. Neither will require the other to do this alone. Deep in my mind I had questions about the proposed death of the healthy one, whichever, but that was what their compact amounted to—the healthy one will arrange for the departure, and then accompany the one who has come to the end of the line.

In the middle ages there was an institution designed to provide a place where one could die with company, and with dignity and a minimum of suffering. It was called Hospice, and the name and the practice have been revived in recent years. Often there is a religious institution involved, but not always. We could call this "organized mythology," perhaps.

Some beautiful things are happening very quietly in Hospice, and one of the most important is the enhancing of the sense of *life*, as people confront Death in full recognition of the fact that we are not in this alone and don't need to go through life thinking that we are. Also, we do not need to die all alone, like dogs in the gutter. The group can be present, physically and in spirit, right up to the moment of departure.

B. The Winner

A dentist took me through his plush and ornately decorated home. He finally led me into his inner sanctum private chamber. There on the wall above his desk, amid all the opulence and ostentation, was a plaque which said, "The kid with the most toys at the end wins." I have thought about that a great deal since then. It may not be important that the owner of the plaque was a dentist, but he was, and I have noticed how the prices of dental work have multiplied alarmingly recently.

"The kid with the most toys at the end wins." I saw the same sentence on a bumper sticker the other day, so the idea is floating around in the public domain, pushed no doubt by those sections of the economy which benefit from gross unthinking consumerism and the amassing of great quantities of toys. Those forces operate the media.

A one-page article in an old issue of **Psychology Today** used a variation of the same slogan as its title: "The One Who Has the Most Toys When He Dies, Wins." The article wasn't about dying at all, but rather about the goals of college students. Let me quote the closing sentences:

> Twenty years ago more than 80 percent of freshmen said that developing a meaningful philosophy of life was an important or essential goal. Today only 41 percent of freshmen consider that goal worthy. Astin and Green note that it could be that making a lot of money precludes the need for a philosophy of life: "It may be that some students view making a lot a money as a kind of philosophy of life in itself."
>
> [May, 1987, p. 54]

The kid with the most toys at the end wins, it says. "Wins

what?" I must ask myself. I'm having trouble here. Is someone giving out prizes, *additional* prizes, to the one who already has the most? Do these people know about something that the rest of us don't? Doesn't "in the end" mean "when you die"? And doesn't that mean no more toys? No nothing. Naked you came into this world, and naked you'll return, to wherever, and with no toys.

Perhaps we can amend the proverb. "The one who dies last wins." Some games are designed around this idea, especially dodge ball and planetary attack computer games. Proponents of hardened bomb shelters for heads of state who can discuss "acceptable losses" in the dozens of millions hold this same belief, no doubt. I must still ask, "Wins *what?*"

"The one who dies with the most toys wins." But it's patently untrue. Whoever dies is out of the game, that is, *loses.* Toys won't keep you from dying. You die anyway. No one has yet been exempted from dying. No one wins, in that sense.

Anyway, aren't toys essentially for infants and children, and those of us who preserve childlike qualities? My observation has been that toys are little fun unless they're shared. The *owners* of the toys did not have the most fun, when I was a kid. Ownership, in fact, was often a last-ditch maneuver in order to be allowed to play. "Yeah, we hafta let *him* play—it's his *ball!*" But that unwanted kid wasn't enjoying himself much.

Jesus told a story, a parable—it's short enough to quote in its entirety.

The land of a rich man brought forth plentifully;
and he thought to himself, "What shall I do, for I have
nowhere to store my crops?" And he said, "I will do
this: I will pull down my barns, and build larger ones;
and there I will store all my grain and my goods. And
I will say to my soul, 'Soul, you have ample goods laid
up for many years; take your ease, eat, drink, be
merry.'" But God said to him, "Fool! This night your
soul is required of you; and the things you have

prepared, whose will they be?"
                    —Luke 12:16b-20 [R.S.V.]

Here's a fellow who doesn't think he has to spend any effort on the question of dying, *his* own pending dying, nor on the meaning of life and the fact that he and we all do die. He lives by the it's-all-mine myth and tends to his wealth, and the implication is plain that *that's* what distracted him from the important questions.

We do not need to spend much time on the Rich Fool. He is not a winner. His notion is infantile, and not recommended for mature persons, no matter how loudly the contemporary media proclaim it. In fact, we have the right to be suspicious of the motives of the media. The more people who are tricked into believing that a human's life consists of the abundance of his possessions, the richer the media hucksters become. Whether their sales pitch is true or not isn't a major concern of theirs. You can tell that from the contents of the ads themselves.

C. Leave Something Behind

Lives of great men all remind us
We can make our lives sublime
And, departing, leave behind us
Footprints on the sands of time
                    —from **The Psalm of Life**, Longfellow

The poet doesn't say so, but one of the implications of his exhortation to amount to something is that if we leave some kind of mark before we go, our going will somehow be more bearable. There are several different ways of attempting this.

"We live on in our children," some have said. I've allowed mine to be weaned, and they're making it fine on their own, and

I'm very proud of the kind of human beings they are. I don't think their lives constitute me in any way—I've tried hard to make sure of that, because of what was done to me and my sisters.

My father quit living his own life, really, and lived vicariously through his children, especially me, the only male offspring. He was quite conscious about it. He had not obeyed God's call; he had not "gone into the ministry," and felt his life was one of disobedience and failure, until the kids came along, late. Then he felt he would get it done, through us. He told me, point blank, after it was all in ruins, that he thought I'd be "some kind of substitute." I told him, "No. Everyone must do his own thing, obey his own call, and make his own lonely journey." I suspect that his awareness that he hadn't done any of those things for himself helped make the end hard for him. Anyway, I'm convinced he lived too much through his children.

So, what shall we make of leaving children behind? Some of our genes are left behind. All three of my children have poor eyesight. One of the three had intolerably crooked teeth. Both defects were inherited from me. It doesn't make me feel good, and doesn't ease the sting of my own mortality. And none of this says anything to those who have no children: the sterile, the nuns, the too ugly or too cantankerous to find partners, the too conscientious to want to add to the already serious problem of overpopulation. The pride some feel about the large numbers of offspring left behind begins to look foolish in the light of world overcrowding.

Leave something behind. Anthropologists claim that this has motivated the artists, from the beginning. Humans know they must die, but they want to leave behind some physical evidence that they were here. So we have cave paintings and megaliths and pyramids and carved marble and oil paintings on canvas—all of which do outlive the artists, albeit only briefly. The breath of the visitors is destroying the cave paintings of thirty thousand years ago; the megaliths and pyramids are eroding away, and modern pollution is pulverizing the statues and the paintings. Yet this attempt to overcome death persists. Graffiti painted on walls and subway cars and carved on tree trunks testify that the efforts are still being made, and not always by skilled artists only.

Not all artists are trying for immortality. Music floats in the air. Poems are heard and forgotten. Books decay faster than most other artifacts. Languages themselves die out, and ours will, too, even if they don't incinerate in an instant all of us who use it along with all our written records.

Empire-builders seem to be trying to overcome Death. Leave something big and important and impressive behind. Live on, by having something named for you—some streets and schools, a continent or two, a tribe, a make of car, a candy bar, a machine gun. Do we really think that Washington and Amerigo and De la Ware and Ford and Hershey and Gatling are any better off, as far as Death is concerned, than all the rest of us?

The destructive inventions, which can be thought of as a kind of art, may be our last desperate attempt to overcome death by the works of our hands. We cannot create life. We can create art. But it is easier to kill and to destroy. We can stop the process itself, on our little planet, which is more than the "Creator" has yet been willing to do, although some myths do state that he's been tempted. We really can do it. The equipment is now in place.

It's the old Tower of Babel pride, gone completely mad. "We'll make a name for ourselves. We'll be the ones who destroyed it all. We'll go down in history," except that History will go down, too. We'll be the first species to destroy itself deliberately. You can't call all this preparation "accidental"! And that will not overcome Death at all. It will be giving Death more than he has coming to him. It'll stop the flow of Life entirely. It'll be the End of the World, with no one left to cheer or hand out any kind of prize.

We need to give Death his due, and choose Life, and live it meanwhile, and share it with each other meanwhile, and leave behind the beautiful creative process as it is, intact. That seems like a stupid thing to have to assert, except that the opposing pride is now so powerful, and so dangerous, that the creative process itself seems to be in danger.

"Leave something behind." A more positive version of this myth can be heard in the phrase, "Leave the world somehow better than you found it." With reference to wilderness, that must mean, "Leave it alone." With reference to human relationships, it can mean, "Leave behind more good will, more mercy and more justice." These abstractions need to be translated into simple concrete actions, and those who have lived that way may find it easier to confront Death, when that day comes.

The need to leave something behind with my name on it is ego. And ego is precisely what makes death hard. My puny little ego—my little glimmer of self-awareness which immediately exaggerates my importance—as soon as I get that under control, this whole thing will be easier.

D. Change Can Be Prevented

Change is afoot in the world, and it always has been. The Wheel of Life is always in motion; the tiny pieces are constantly being moved, rearranged in a new kaleidoscopic pattern. The frame of Real Life never freezes; the pattern is never ever stopped and fixed. Heraklitus, the Greek philosopher, stated clearly that Reality is Flux, and that everything is in motion. "You can't step into the same river twice," he said. No one has ever refuted him.

Joseph Campbell, in **Hero with a Thousand Faces**, describes the Hero as the agent, or representative, of the pending change. Guardians of the old way—meaning the way it is and has been, the establishment, the status quo—do not like change. They resist change, and oppose the ideas that lead to change. In mythology these forces are represented as Hold-Fast, the evil ogre/monster/ruler. Hold-Fast wants to stop the Wheel.

There is a little of Hold-Fast is all of us, I think. We keep trying to hang on to something, to stop the clock, to hinder that relentless flow of time and life, because we can feel Life Itself dribbling through our fingers. We're not sure that all change is progress—in fact, we're pretty sure it isn't. They tore down the little town I grew up in and built a freeway, for instance. The evolution of war weapons in modern times, from muzzle-loader, to bolt-action rifle, to machine gun, from cannonball, to bombs, to nuclear explosives—those changes have hardly been for the better for anybody. Many of us wish we could go back to the time before those things existed, but we cannot.

Part of the panic felt by many elderly people has to do with this change business, and the accelerated pace of change that we are now in the middle of. Communication is instantaneous and nine-tenths of the news is bad. The noise is constant, mostly from motors. The computers have taken over, but they go awry and can't be comprehended or corrected. There is poison in everything. Unheard-of freedoms and over choice are available to the young, compared to the options offered us fifty years ago. It is too much change, and too fast. We wish we could find a way to stop it, or a place somewhere, where it could be prevented.

It's an old idea, found in all the religions of the world. Go inside yourself there and find that quiet silent center, the unmoved center around which everything gyrates, that unchangeable spot. Some want to call it "God." Flight from change accounts for much of the motivation for this exercise.

> Change and decay in all around I see—
> Oh, Thou, that changest not, abide with me.

But the search for the Unchangeable is hopeless. Nothing abides. Heraklitus was right. It *will* change. It *is now changing.*

The yearning for no-change makes people conservative, and even reactionary. Let's go back to when there were no atomic weapons or atomic power plants and no atomic waste material with a half-life longer than the age of humanity. Let's dismantle all that. Let's not cut down all the trees. Let's leave Antarctica unchanged. Let's not kill the last elephant. Let's preserve the wilderness, as it is. There's something appealing, and even correct, about this attitude. It is tragic that Alaska is being changed from a wild-life preserve into an oil slick.

But all that yearning has to be funneled into *influencing* the pending changes, not trying to prevent change itself, which is a hopeless task. Not all change is bad, anyway. But it is wearisome and annoying to have to run always, "just to keep up."

> New occasions teach new duties,
> Time makes ancient good uncouth;
> They must ever up and onward
> Who would keep abreast of truth.
> —from **The Crisis**, James Russell Lowell

"Just as I learn the game, they change the rules."

"I learned how to do that, just as I finished the last one."

"Now that I've figured out the answers, they've changed the questions."

"I can't even imagine all the possibilities."

The yearning for the Good Old Days is part weariness, part faulty memory, and part awareness that some changes have not been for the better. But it is hopeless. The Good Old Days never were, and they're not coming back.

I knew a man who tried very hard not to change. He resisted and lamented all the changes around him. He regarded the first decade of the last century as correct and "normal," and evaluated everything by comparing it to the way things were then: strawberries priced at three cents a box, poor and dark-skinned people kept in their proper places, women at home raising children and cooking and sewing, Republicans in charge of the political system.

He often cried out, "Don't change it!" He meant variations on a piece of music on the piano, or the words of a song, and even the TV channel in the late stages of his life. "Don't change it!" The strange thing about it all was, the more he *didn't* change, the more out of step he became, the more unreasonable, the more difficult to live with. His *not* changing constituted a kind of change itself.

A middle-aged woman complained to her sister, "You keep changing! You change what you believe—you quit going to church. You took a job. You moved away. You divorced! You keep changing!"

"Yes," the sister replied. "I'm changing. I'm on the move, not stuck. Not glued to the past, not mired in the old arrangement of things. I'm sorry if that means you're not allowed to like me or support me. But I can't stay the way I was, stuck in that situation, just to make you feel more comfortable. I'm changing, all right. *You* should try it!"

Some parents rear their children in a more or less constant state of alarm, for fear that the children will change. But they *will* change, if they're healthy and growing. "They read those awful books, with all those new and dangerous ideas. We should keep those books away from them. They experience new things that I never dreamed of and can't understand. They have minds of their own. They reason for themselves! They change their minds! They reject my ideas. They grow up!" But would you want it otherwise? Do you really want clones for children?

A congregation in a back-water community kept their eager and ambitious young pastor constantly frustrated, by countering every proposal he made with the refrain, "We never did *that* before." Church and pastor never got together on anything.

Entropy comes to mind. Things fall apart. It freezes. It gets out of tune. It disintegrates. The roof begins to leak. The drain becomes stopped up. The shoes wear out. Young rugged mountains become old, worn-down mountains. Stars explode. Weeds and cobwebs overgrow everything. But that at least means that growth is also going on. In addition to the plants you think you don't like and the spiders and the bacteria of putrefaction, that tree you planted decades ago is now taller than the house.

Change cannot be prevented. And now to our theme—there's that Big Change pending. "No being soever, born or created, can overcome the tendency to dissolution inherent in itself. A condition of permanence is impossible." The Buddha said that to his disciple, Amanda, chiding him, because Amanda was mourning the Buddha's immanent passage into Nirvana, which will look like dying to any outside observer.

E. It's No Good to Be Old

The story-telling media in our country never wander far from one unrelenting theme: "It's no good to be old."

The television stories and pictures, and the magazine covers and articles and pictures, tell all of us at every turn of the page, through every button on the remote, "Young is beautiful, and agile and good, while age is none of these things." It's a variation of the myth that change can be prevented.

The poet W. B. Yeats didn't invent this myth, and the believers and perpetrators of it in our day probably are not great fans of his poetry either, yet he did put it into marvelous words, some while ago:

The Land of Heart's Desire
... where nobody gets old and godly and grave,
... where nobody gets old and crafty and wise,
... where nobody gets old and bitter of tongue.

Our story-telling media are trying to tell us that we all can live, and do our getting and spending, in this always youthful Land of Heart's Desire, where aging is not taking place. It is a lie.

In fact, the very idea that there's something wrong with being old is absurd. It makes every single last one of us a loser, because every one of us, and of them, too, is in the process of *becoming* old, or older, at all times, and at exactly the same rate.

The myth creates a lower class of citizens, the old, in spite of the incontrovertible fact that without exception everyone alive is moving inexorably into that class. You're not born into it, the way you can be born black or brown or female. And it's not a class you can work your way out of, one way or another maybe, like poverty. No, but it's a class that absolutely every survivor will end up *in*. So, why are we letting them set up prejudices and obstacles and hindrances for a class that you can only stay out of in one way?

All persons born seventy or more years ago are either old or dead. A young reporter asked a very old man what he thought of old age, what with slower and reduced activity and the accompanying aches and pains. "I wonder about it sometimes," he replied, "until I think of the alternative."

Nevertheless, the myths, the stories, the pictures, the images all say, "Youth is beautiful," implying at the same time that age is not. There are no come-on pictures of nude, or nearly nude, elderly people. Those pictures are of smooth-skinned supple-limbed, lean and lanky youths. There are massive advertising campaigns ballyhooing that youthful thinness. The fact that humans tend to become heavier, especially around the middle, as they reach middle age is posed as a problem which the young salespersons can solve, with diets, special foods, ointments, pills, and expensive exercise programs.

"Why grow old gracefully?" they ask, implying that you shouldn't, that you should use their products instead. But growing old ungracefully, which is the only real alternative, doesn't sound like such a good idea either. We are all unavoidably growing old, one way or another. Why fight it? And why pretend we're not?

Most of the talk and songs and images suggest that it's best to be young. And then, when you can't be young, you can pretend to be. A "breakthrough" was announced recently—a cream that removes wrinkles. One delighted user said that it subtracted years from his life. Another stated that it added years! Both meant, we may presume, that the cream removed wrinkles. The first user looked younger than he knew he was, so he said the cream subtracted years. The other also looked younger than he was, but he was fooled into thinking that that meant he would live longer, so he called the process addition. In both cases it was not arithmetic, but deception. Another wiser user suspected the wrinkle-free cream was an irritant that caused swelling of the skin, thus unwrinkling the wrinkles.

Persons who need to appear to be younger than they are have given this questionable myth too much power. Youth may be beautiful, but youth is also inexperienced and unaware and not yet wise.

It's true that some youth are smarter than we were at that age, but they are not smarter than our perspective and experience make us now. And, poor things, they are forced to make long-range, far-reaching decisions without that perspective and experience. Don't believe it, that it's best to be young. We know better. I wouldn't trade places with the young for anything. The fact is, I feel a little bit sorry for them, and I sure don't need to look like them or pretend I still am one of them.

It takes a lot of guts to be old. Not everyone makes it. There are some aspects of it which I frankly like very much. The notion of equality, for one thing, which we think is so very American, is something I've only been able to appreciate personally in these later stages. Sometime after I turned forty, and more so after fifty, I found I no longer had to defer to my elders. Now past seventy I've become one of the elders, and I can make my case without wondering whether maybe I should be quiet and let the wiser experienced ones have all the say. I can have my say, too.

I've been told by persons older than I that it is a great relief, finally, to be allowed to express oneself. "Oh, they don't *listen*. They just say I'm a crazy old lady. But at least I get to say what I really think!" And I believe, as we become more and better organized, the rest of them will yet have to listen and pay more attention to what we think.

Some are already beginning to feel and fear the political clout of AARP. Some forces have used that clout, with deleterious effect. I'm thinking of the recent disastrous changes in Medicare, which were supposed to provide help with prescriptions for the elderly, but turned into a bonanza for HMO's and pharmaceutical corporations, with little real help for the patients. AARP needs to use its growing clout very carefully.

One important aspect about getting older is that we're confronted with a narrowing range of possibilities. We pass by gates in life, pass them by for ever, and some of them we pass by early. "I'll never be a professional football player, after all." I remember seeing that clearly more than fifty years ago. Maybe that's just silly, a stupid ambition at best, one might say, but it became a symbol for me of my awareness of this fact. I have a slightly crazy desire to do everything, to try everything. It's ridiculous and impossible, and my awareness of my own aging is making that clear, and giving me relief. You can't do everything, Harry. Do this, and this, and do them well, and rest content. I am finding relief from over choice, which is a plague troubling many of our young people. The shutting down of options allows fresh concentration on what I more and more urgently do want to do—write this book, for instance. Do it, Harry. Quit flying around in all directions, pretending you're a ballerina.

The waning level of energy, which many fear, and many lament and some become angry about when they experience it—I must say I have found it a gift. I'm learning that it's all right to rest. I have become addicted to the afternoon nap. Extra unspent energy, what some wise persons have called "disposable libido," causes so much of the trouble and heartache of the earlier stages of life. I know about that. I have learned to be glad for the waning, and for the control which results. Memories are far less threatening and dangerous than continuing in the middle of that mad frenzy.

Age is beautiful, even if our current myths don't say so. Other cultures have known it, and we have a minority report which indicates it clearly. I love to study photographs of the faces of the old and wallow in the wrinkles. I am in awe of that long, long view that only the old can have. Patience is beautiful, experience is beautiful, wisdom is beautiful. The longer perspective has its satisfactions, as it develops in us with age. The stock market crash of 1987 was not so hard on those who could remember the previous one, even though the youngsters on Wall Street thought the sky was falling. It is remarkable how easily they forgot it again, and so we had the bubble-bursting 90's.

This youth-obsession is a questionable myth to live by or to organize a society by. I, for one, have chucked it, and I now refuse to think of my life as a race against time. Instead, time is a flow that we are all in. We don't need any expensive illusions that pretend to assure us that the flow isn't flowing.

Our culture wants to put the old ones out to pasture, on the shelf, out of the way, and off the job market. That last is an important clue, as if there weren't enough meaningful tasks to go around! There is an indication here about our culture's basic values. Soldiering, with all the violence it entails, is for young people. Teaching, remembering, seeing long-range connections, telling stories based on wise experience—all that is for older people. And our culture still prefers soldiering—look at that budget! We appear to be content to throw away great quantities of both experience and wisdom.

I've noticed how much better off we'd be if our country's foreign policy, for example, could be determined by a committee of *former* secretaries of state and secretaries of defense, even those who were ravenous warmongers when they were in office. They mellow, without exception; they develop perspective. They begin to think globally and consider mankind as a species and care more about the global environment; they are less into personal, or even national, self-aggrandizement.

There is no avoiding the one great truth about age. Death looms. I wonder whether my recent more or less continual observation of that fact could be turning me into what Yeats disliked about growing old. "Old and godly and grave, ... old and crafty and wise, ... old and bitter of tongue." I'm leery of "godly;" it depends on the definition of "God." A little bit of "grave" is plenty, and I don't like the feel of "crafty." "Wise" I like. I certainly hope this exercise isn't making me "bitter of tongue." But at any rate, "old" must be faced.

The poet Dylan Thomas felt that "facing it" should include some sense of helpless fury. His most famous poem is addressed to his elderly father:

> Do not go gentle into that good night,
> Old age should burn and rave at close of day,
> Rage, rage against the dying of the light.

In his own life he burned and raved in the middle of the day, and never reached old age. He died at age thirty-nine, with repeated self-inflicted doses of alcohol. If he was in such a rage about going into the night, why would he extinct himself at such an early age? It's a puzzle.

Dylan Thomas didn't know old age from personal experience, but only by observation, and he could not handle the ability of some elderly people to accept the dying of the light and go gentle. His own middle-aged rage confused him and he was simply wrong about old age. This poem is probably not about old age and what should happen "at close of day" anyway. More likely it's about something personal and mysterious between him and his father. At any rate, it is a poem expressing the feelings of the one being left, not the one dying.

Death, and the growing awareness of it, can sweeten age. It doesn't always, but it can. *This* moment becomes so precious. There is less inclination to waste so many of these valuable moments. There is more awareness and more sensitivity; more nerve endings are functioning, in my experience of it, not fewer. We older people know we won't live forever, and I find when we really think about it, we wouldn't want to. We'd rather live, to the hilt, until the great interruption.

A cup of cold water, a flower, the sunshine, the warmth of a fire—these little things become the best things. A touch—it can be as precious, and as full of meaning, as the old erotic marathon romp ever was.

It's not true that only the old die, but it is more likely that oldsters will be aware that it's coming. Some dare prepare and then live thankfully meanwhile. Logan P. Smith, the fellow who first commented that the pen is mightier than the sword, also had some wise observations about Death and age:

> Why are happy people not afraid of Death, while the insatiable and the unhappy so abhor that grim feature?
>
> What with its crude awakenings can youth know of the rich return of awareness to elderly people from their afternoon naps; of their ironic thoughts and long retrospections, and the sweetness they taste of not being dead?

There are some marvelously wonderful things about being old, and as we become more aware of them, we'll be less likely to allow ourselves to be relegated to a class of second-rate citizens.

ɜ▲

F. The Man Upstairs

Persons who know nothing of philosophy or theology, and who stay away from churches as a general rule, can be caught referring to "The Man Upstairs" with an upward roll of the eyeballs. It's a myth, a metaphor, and not a very good one, even though it is popular in contemporary stories. "The Man Upstairs" is usually described as very wise, perhaps all-knowing. He keeps track, like a Cosmic Bookkeeper. He tends to things, somehow. It is not a good metaphor, because there is no "upstairs" to it, and whatever is being referred to, it is not a man.

The Man Upstairs refers to "God," without any traditional theological content. Usually what is meant is that "God" is smarter, has a better perspective and more control of things than we downstairs ordinary mortals. There is seldom much ethical content to this Man Upstairs—I wonder what he thinks of nuclear stockpiling, cruelty, hypocrisy, or leaders who lie. When the old prophets talked about "The Lord God," you knew what *that* God thought about such subjects.

Perhaps we should simply dismiss this myth as worthless and move on, but I sense that there are some important clues hidden here. Why would people be tempted to want to use a metaphor in which "God" is referred to as The Man Upstairs? I submit that it is because they want a God they can handle, and maybe even one they can deceive. I refer to him as "Dim-witted God," and even *"Dios Pendejo,"* in my book, **Freedom from God: Restoring the Sense of Wonder**.

The modern obsession with secrecy is an expression of this. If there is an all-seeing, all-wise Deity watching and comprehending all things, why so much effort at deception? Presidents and military cabinet persons are upset about "leaks" and "publicity." They are terrified of the media. They work hard to prevent the discovery and dissemination of truth and they have formed Departments of Disinformation. The press must be controlled, they say. Future wars will not be fought on television, they say, as if by hiding it, wars and bombings could be made into something that good people would approve of.

At the same time, these public officials talk a great deal about "God." They usually pronounce the syllable with a very flat "a", making a weak sound, revealing, inadvertently, that their "God" is also weak. What kind of God do these hiders and deceivers have? Is he blind, after all? Is he not just, after all? Is he not Truth, after all? And if so, who cares at all about such a God, really?

The same thing surfaces closer to home. I know a lady who believes in God, yet she still tries to hide the fact that her husband steals, that her daughter is on dope, and that she herself has cancer. Who is she hiding all this truth from? Me? Herself, more likely. What about "God"? What about The Man Upstairs?

One valuable insight is this: "God" is another metaphor. There is no Creator, in the sense that one part of What-There-Is made all the rest, and rules it or runs it, and can be identified and then appealed to. It is not a case of Creator/Creation, after the analogy of Potter/Pot. We do not live in that kind of universe. It is all one world, all One Thing, with all the parts interconnected. And "God" could be a metaphor for THAT, all of That, all of What-There-Is-As-It-Is. But usually people don't use the word "God" to mean that at all.

You can see why The Man Upstairs is such a paltry metaphor. "God" isn't even enough, not big enough, not inclusive enough. "God" is too tangled up with preposterous notions, relics of old myths, like robes and beards and thunderbolts and thrones and naked flying cherubs. J. B. Phillips wrote an excellent book fifty years ago—the title alone is worth the price: **Your God Is Too Small**.

Someone asked me recently, "Don't you believe in God?"

I answered, "If you insist on a monosyllabic answer, without my knowing in what sense you mean the metaphor, then my answer must be, 'No.' That's on the assumption that either you mean the metaphor in a way that I do not believe, or that you deny that there is any metaphor to it.

"But, if I may give a multi-syllabic and multi-paragraph answer, I'll say this. 'God' can be a metaphor for All There Is, What There Is, The Cosmos, The Cosmic Process, All of Reality. I prefer not to use the metaphor. The circumlocutions, with faltering and fumbling inadequate language, richly peppered with '-um-' and '-er-' and 'OM!' is better.

"I do like to think and try to talk about 'all of it.' I believe it is important that humans do so. The metaphor hinders, however, because it is too easy to use. The little word pops out, even as a cuss word, with no meaning, or almost no meaning, or a false meaning derived from the metaphor itself and not from what the metaphor refers to.

"People who prate about 'God' seldom think about 'What There Is,' or 'All There Is As It Is,' or 'The Oneness of What Is,' or 'The Intention or Purpose or Meaning or Whatever of the Whole Cosmic Process.' They're thinking about a father or a king or a lord of the manor or maybe a potter—some small part of the Cosmic Whole, and what special advantages can come to them through being on 'his side.' Particle physicists and astronomers, some of them, some of whom never ever say, 'God,' come closer to the kind of thinking I believe we need a great deal more of."

The person who asked me backed away before I was finished explaining myself. I could see her thinking, "Ask a simple question and get a pageant for an answer!"

"We just hope God understands," the mother said to the TV reporter and his audience, as they gave their hopelessly deformed stillborn baby's organs away. It was thought-provoking, not only the moral dilemma the woman felt she was in, but the myth she was using. "Maybe God doesn't understand," she plainly implied.

Imagine—a God who doesn't understand. It comes from taking the metaphor of the man upstairs seriously, or literally. But "God" ought not to mean that old man up there who may or may not understand. "God" should mean Reality. What There Is, As IT Is. IT is consistent with itself, and entirely in touch with itself. So that means that IT understands, more dependably than "God" or any humanly contrived metaphor. You can depend on IT to understand.

I can't be certain, but frankly I suspect that it would be best for humans to search for more clarity on this before the last minute. Delivering one's "soul" to "God" at the end of life—what does that really mean, with neither term defined or even thought about? There's a lot at stake, to be content to take the priest's or pastor's word for it. And how does *he* know? Isn't this something that each one should do for himself or herself?

"Delivering one's soul to God" can be a very fine metaphor. It can mean that the dying person believes that the Cosmos is a safe place, that I accept my mortal limitations, that I have given living a good try, that it was "worth it." It can even mean that I believe that whatever is on the other side, if anything, will be good for me, just as life has been. But I need more than The Man Upstairs to assure me of that. I need galaxies and evolution and black holes and electrons and osmosis and heat and light and consciousness and will and love.

"God" seems inadequate, frankly. How about "The Undeviating Justice"? Now there's a phrase. The old alchemists used it. Isaac Newton tried to make mathematics of the idea. Pendulums can illustrate it. Everything comes out even in the end. It is all recorded, in the endless chain of connections. Nobody gets away with anything. No loopholes, no exceptions, no extenuating circumstances, but rather The Undeviating Justice.

This is a tough doctrine. Yet alchemists claimed to believe it, and to work wonders by means of it. Heavier-than-air machines fly, not in spite of the law of gravity, but because of an improved understanding of that very law. Alchemists operated on the same principle. If you know How-It-Is, you can do wonders. But The Undeviating Justice is a far cry from The Man Upstairs.

Nevertheless it can be believed, believed in, understood—more and more fully. The problem is, it requires a longer view, a very much longer view than one short little human ego-centered lifetime.

This becomes a little scary. In the East they call it Karma—you get what's coming to you. And whatever you get, you had it coming to you. If you do believe in this stuff, it'll make you put your life in order. Believing in "God" *should* do that, one would think, but notice how often it doesn't.

A North American church group was studying Central America and the cause of all the unhappiness there. One member expressed himself with striking honesty. "I used to believe in equality. But now that I've learned how much my life-style depends on the uneven distribution of the world's goods, I don't believe in it anymore." One must assume, also, that he doesn't believe in some Divine Cosmic Force, like "God" or The Undeviating Justice, which will even things out sooner or later.

It may be easier for members of blatantly oppressed groups to believe in The Undeviating Justice. For straight white male imperialist Americans I suspect it may have an unpleasant ring to it. I know I definitely feel that. Thomas Jefferson felt something similar, looking at slavery and foreseeing what we now call the Civil War almost forty years in advance: "I tremble for my country when I remember that God is just," referring, I take it, to The Undeviating Justice.

I'd like to think that I believe in and accept the dispositions of Pure Cosmic Justice, but my paltry little ego whimpers in doubt. I watched this go wrong for my father. As Judgement Day loomed, for him, he quailed. He hadn't tended to ego, and it needs to be tended to, before the last minute.

❧❧❧❧❧

VII

STORIES FROM SOCIO-POLITICAL MOVEMENTS

Some people live very consciously and deliberately by their myths. Their belief systems determine what they want, what they do with their time and talent, how they feel, what they care about. Others seem to be less clear about it. What they say they believe doesn't seem to affect how they live. They may be fooling themselves about what they believe. What a person really believes can be inferred by observing his or her life.

It is interesting to watch this carefully. Some persons say, with considerable fervor, that they believe in God, and when asked will state that God is Just, that he cares about Justice and in the long run executes Justice. Then I notice that these same persons are gung-ho to throw napalm and sulphur bombs on little children. They send money to organized criminals, called "contras," in the case of Nicaragua in the 1980's, who commit gang rape on nurses and day care center personnel.

I suspect that some of the contradictions I have observed are the unconscious result of persons being deceived by word games and lying and government disinformation and official contamination of the language. But I'm convinced that some of it is deliberate. Some of the people who talk the longest and the loudest about "God" don't really believe in anything and are assuming that there really is no such thing as a just God.

Nevertheless, it is possible, and even advisable, to examine one's life and one's professed belief system at the same time, with hope of getting them into line. "Why don't you preach what you practice?" the Presbyterians used to ask the Quakers, whose acts were blatant demonstrations of love and mercy while at the same time they seemed a little vague about doctrinal matters.

I know people who are gentle, utterly honest, completely just in their actions and their estimates of others, careful to be absolutely fair in their analysis of what others do and say, and these same persons do not profess to believe in much of anything. They are even a little suspicious of mythology, because of the rampant hypocrisy which receives all the attention and the headlines. Yet they do have a mythology. They believe in Justice. They believe in Truth. They don't know why they have this inclination to support those who have been betrayed and cheated and lied to, but they have it and they act on it. To me in private, they question whether the world even makes sense, and then they proceed to pour as much sense, and love, into their lives and all the human connections they have as they possibly can. So what do they believe? Perhaps it's commendable not to believe so much, not to pretend to be so sure about these things.

Some of the many stories, beliefs and metaphors which surround us came originally from social groups and political movements. We need to look at them and evaluate them.

A. Our Country Is Best

A very dangerous myth has grown frightfully strong in recent years. "Our country is best." It's one thing for a people to say, "Our country is all right. We don't know which is the best, but this is the one we're in, and we're proud to be part of it, and we want to improve it, in any way we can."

It's a different thing for a people to say, "We are superior. We are better. They are inferior. We love our homes and children and they do not. We deserve to lord it over them. They are barbarians. We value human life, and they don't. Life is cheap there." The name of this myth is nationalism, and it moves quickly to that last assertion, that life is cheap in other places, in order to justify the destruction of so many lives.

The origin of the word "barbarian" gives it all away. It was the Greek word for all persons who spoke one of the several thousand human languages that were not Greek. It really means "Everybody Else." They used it then, and now everybody uses it, to mean, "Someone we have the right to conquer or kill."

Nationalism leads to wars of aggression, covert operations, deception and outright blatant lies as part of national policy. The myth of superiority must be taught to the soldiers and sailors, to the draftees, to the wounded, to the families of the fallen, and to the survivors. It spreads to the teachers, the history teachers even, who should know better, and the youth, who will furnish additional recruits. The old ones become inclined to be a little cynical about all this, but they also tend to say little and so the myth is propagated far and wide, more and more. TV commentators, sports announcers, especially at the quadrennial Olympic Games, and those story-tellers who have access to the media—all tend to use this myth to fill the minds of their viewers. Politicians fall back on it, even when they know better, when the lies are so blatant we think they'll choke—still they insist that this country is the best. But the most powerful is not the best. The most powerful may well be the most responsible, but that is not the same thing.

This is a very poor myth to live by, or to die by, because it is patently false. All one has to do is study some history, and think about whatever topic may be of interest, from the angle of the other group. Try the point of view of the Mohicans, or the Aztecs, or the Mandingo, or the Poles, or the Armenians, or the Koreans, or the Nicaraguans, or the Iranians, for starters.

Nationalism is a force which sucks up huge portions of every government budget, and has become so armed with weapons of overkill, that people talk nowadays of the End of the World, and they don't mean that branch of mythology called eschatology—the study of the "last things." The end of the world, the close of the age, the conclusion of the imperial dynasty, the end of the republic—all the world's mythologies have stories about the end. Now we have them, too. We wonder whether the ocean can be kept alive, whether or not it's too late to save the living environment, whether humanity itself is one of the "endangered species" on this planet.

In our time people have tried to distance themselves from the impending danger by saying that it's no different now than when humans first invented the bow and arrow, or gunpowder. But our times are unique. We really are approaching the end of many things, many species, and the evidence now is not merely "myth."

We are coming to the end, not of one particular civilization, which happens all the time, but the end of civilization itself. We are coming to the end, and we're threatening to take with us that very flow of life and events which we used to call "history." Our departure threatens that life process, which we have labeled "evolution." No other collapsing civilization ever posed such a threat to the basic processes which underlie everything.

We are ready to defend "our way of life," at the cost of the future of history and evolution, "our country," which we think is best, "our civilization," which we think is superior. But all that is doomed. All civilizations have always been short-lived. Our existence as a species is doomed, also, and has been from the beginning. Every species is. But the destruction of life-forms, all of them, is a new thing, which now looms somewhere between the very likely and the inevitable.

Consider: poisoned fresh water, poisoned ocean, nuclear fire-power and nuclear waste some of which will be lethal for 250,000 years, exhausted mines and farms, lost top soil, limited energy supplies, increasing mutual hostility, degenerating ozone layer, drastically diminished rain forest, the greenhouse effect and melting polar ice caps, ever rapidly doubling world population, genetic meddling, chemical/biological weapons, new plagues. Our refusal to deal with these perceived threats to Life Itself pushes us nearer to inevitability.

Christians have a myth about the End of the World. Unclear passages in the Book of Revelation hint at a glorious battle in the future on the Plain of Armageddon. That spot in northern Israel is the site of the Battle of Megiddo. King Josiah of Judah, whose career began with great hopes and plans for reform triggered by the discovery of the Book of Deuteronomy, became involved in empire-building wars between Egypt and Assyria. At Megiddo he was defeated by Pharaoh Neco, and killed, in 608 B.C. The whole story surely sounds vaguely familiar, reminding thoughtful persons of how LBJ's plans for the Great Society drowned in the Gulf of Tonkin, his excuse for the Vietnam war.

In the apocalyptic myth of Armageddon, God supposedly will ring down the curtain on human history itself, in the last great battle. The details, right there in the text, are extremely unclear. Check the last several chapters of the last book of the Bible. People who know exactly which 21st-century forces each name or number or symbol refers to in this section are liars. It would in fact be comical, except for the fact that the wherewithal to conclude history and destroy all life forms on the planet is now in place, and some of the persons in charge of the use of that wherewithal seem to take literally this Armageddon material. More than twenty thousand nuclear warheads, and the resulting nuclear winter—it is not possible to exaggerate how serious the threat of the End of the World really is.

Dying is a lonely act. Everyone does it alone, we're used to saying. Everyone can do it to the tune of his own myth, and should be free to do so. But I must admit to not approving of letting my life and "my" world and "my" oxygen supply and "my" access to sun's rays and photosynthesis be sucked into someone else's myth to die by. Nationalists who believe that arrogant nonsense about Armageddon are free to believe whatever they like. But let's keep their hands off of nuclear trigger-buttons and their noses out of super-power summits.

Self-fulfilling prophecies are not adequate myths to die by either.

The Armageddon myth is used by living madmen to say that evil forces will destroy the world. The myth itself says that God will destroy it. Truth seems to be warning that if we're not very careful, we'll destroy it ourselves. "We have met the enemy, and he is us."

If God wants to destroy the world, I guess we'll have to let him, if there is a God. But let us not be the ones who destroy the world. Let's get rid of the wherewithal. We can't afford it, for one thing, and we don't want to destroy the world, anyway, do we?

What can an individual human do in such times as these? Try to be a part of the solution, not part of the problem. Drop nationalism forthwith as a value to live by or die for. Think in planetary terms. Devote your love and loyalty to the Biosphere. Seek ways of saying, "No," to the violence, the corrupted values, the mindless, thoughtless, cynical greed. Try to be the kind of human being who ought not to be extincted. And plan meanwhile on being out of step with the vast majority.

When I share these kinds of thoughts with the people around me, some of them tell me I am overly pessimistic. "Life will find a way," my son says. I hope he is right. This experiment with living beings on this beautiful planet ought not to be concluded, just because some nationalists are too proud to think straight. I notice that his statement implies a time scale that does not include nations, or even species. Another friend told me that he thought that some bacteria hidden deep in solid rocks "will survive what's pending, and the whole thing can start over."

B. Male Is Superior

"You've come a long way, Baby," may be true, but there's still a way to go. Full-grown persons willing to be called "Baby" may be a clue, for starters. At any rate, it hardly needs saying that the notion that females are inferior, in any way, is not a myth for any of us, male or female, to take seriously.

The authoritative statements that support this myth are derived from old patriarchal religions. The Hebrew tradition stated that the woman was the property of the man, first the father and then the husband. Both the Christian and Islamic faiths built on this foundation. "Wives, be subject to your husbands." The custom of the father giving the bride away as part of the wedding ceremony harks back to this. Actually, in many cases it would be more accurate to say he's selling her, what with dowries and bride prices and all that. One wonders how any self-respecting modern woman could allow herself to be "given away."

Thankfully, all that is crumbling in our day, but it's been a hard struggle and it isn't completed yet. Not long ago women couldn't hold title to property. Community property does not yet hold true in all states in the USA. The Founding Fathers didn't think women should vote. Divorce was impossible not long ago, and then difficult. It still tends to be a financial disaster for the woman. Her skill and effort in the marketplace are still not rewarded fairly. Vast numbers of the unaware still question whether we should, and marvel that we do, have women as judges, doctors, ambassadors, congresspersons, mail carriers, astronauts, coal miners, cab drivers and corporation executives.

I remember years ago teaching a class of seventh graders about the division of labor in the primitive Cro-Magnon human family. "Well, why was it that the female ended up being the one who stayed with the cubs and became keeper of the fire?"

"She had the mammary glands!" one young lady declared. "But that doesn't mean he shouldn't stick around and help!"

I agreed. And now the old roles are shifting. I have been part of a little role-reversal myself, and must say I've learned much that is important and have experienced much that did me good, while being fun at the same time. Men can cook, and wash the dishes and sort the clothes and change the diapers. In our family we laugh about it all—my wife insists she has no interest in taking over the rototilling! But she could!

A study of the so-called patriarchal and matriarchal values can be very helpful. The male, in the culture which has been traditional but is now waning, or changing, was the one who expressed aggression, who was interested in power and rank, who made rules and demands and qualifications. The father's love, traditionally, was conditional, depending on the response and the obedience and the subservience of the beloved. The matriarchal values were those of nurturing, giving without stint or return, accepting and allowing equality among all the offspring. The mother's love was unconditional, offered to all her offspring no matter what.

We need both sets of values, although we are near to overdosing on patriarchy at the moment. The Pentagon Budget, citizens with no health insurance or care, the homeless, the hungry—all these problems testify to the overdoing of the patriarchal values.

There are lessons in the symbols for male and female. The arrow, symbol of Mars, is the male symbol. It is a weapon. It creates change, it puts things in motion, it is active.

The mirror, symbol of Venus, is the female symbol. It is a circle with a cross beneath, and is itself a symbol for the whole world, the unity of the world, the Oneness, the all-inclusive power, the tendency to connect things, the roundness, the cycles of nature, the eternal return.

To make one half of Reality inferior to another is plainly silly. Yang is not superior to Yin. All of Reality is both, and each part must partake of both. A typical "retirement" story illustrates this:

Phil worked long hard hours all his life, outside the home. He never did much else, really, besides work, and rest in the evenings and on weekends. Then he retired. He had nothing to do —no hobbies, no creative projects; he didn't read, didn't have any kind of do-it-yourself business he wanted to get into. So what did he do? He got into Sally's business—grocery shopping, housecleaning, shopping for furniture and appliances, supervising children, that is, grandchildren. Sally was furious. All that used to be *her* territory! He thought she was a nag, because she was indeed becoming one. He needed to get his own thing going, and quickly—woodworking, photography, painting, ceramics, basketry, written memoirs—

When the division of labor is too rigid, problems can result. When one thinks the other is inferior, in this day and age, trouble is certain.

I've been called a feminist, by women activists, and I'm proud of the label. Equality is my thing, really, and I do think it would do us good as a group to pay a great deal more attention to the matriarchal values. In fact, we are doomed, if we don't.

Machismo is becoming passé. A local Spanish proverb states, "He who worries about his machismo probably needs to." I watch with a mixture of sadness and gladness the almost common sight of a young woman going to the University, discovering her *brain*, finding herself in the world with talent and energy, and her perplexed young macho husband, losing her, because he can't keep her barefoot and pregnant, and doesn't understand or follow all she's learning. She's on her way, and he and his machismo have been left behind.

What does all this have to do with dying? Well, I wonder why women tend to live longer than men. Is the macho life-style, which is essentially battle and stress on all fronts, more damaging in the long run? Is nurturing a skill which redounds on the nurturer, after many decades? So many elderly men seem so utterly helpless, whereas most women learned to take care of themselves, and others, long ago. I'm not sure what can be proved by longevity statistics, but the indication seems clear that machismo is not a myth to live by, and is poor preparation for the later stages of life.

ی&

C. Necrophilia

The word necrophilia comes from Greek and means "love of death." It originally referred to a sexual perversion, which involved sexual attraction to corpses. The newspapers refer to a certain crime as "rape/murder," but it would be more correct chronologically sometimes, if they called it "murder/rape"—the diseased person commits murder in order to have a corpse to rape.

Extreme acted-out instances of this perversion are comparatively rare. Erich Fromm in his book, **The Heart of Man**, wanted to expand the use of the term "necrophilia" beyond this technical meaning. What he termed the necrophilous orientation is so widespread that we must consider it as part of our study of myth and mortality. It has pathological roots and infects young and old, unsung and famous. It seems especially prevalent among decision-makers in positions of power in many nations. It is "love of death," fascination with death, preference for death over life.

The person with the necrophilous orientation is attracted to and fascinated by what is not alive—corpses, decay, feces, stones, dirt, and mechanical processes rather than organic ones. Such a person loves control, order, certainty and force, and dislikes or is afraid of the spontaneity, rich variety, ambiguity and general messiness typical of living things.

In our time there is a kind of fascinated eagerness to play with death. "Chicken" is the name of a game played with motorized vehicles hurtling toward each other at great speed. Those of us not playing must simply yield on the highways of our country. Auto racing, as a "sport," has some of this quality in it, for drivers and for watchers. We no longer have gladiators fighting to the death to entertain us, but besides auto racing, we have boxing, which is a modified form of playing with death.

Playing football on a concrete surface is hardly any better. Russian roulette, so-called and misnamed, claims victims every now and then, even right here in our home town.

We have come to be entranced, and then just a little bored, by the pictures of violence and death on the evening news, and the most popular TV programs fictionalize the violence and the dying and multiply the instances of violent images that enter the minds and memories and dream processes of the viewers.

I have questioned teenagers who liked Rambo movies and vice in Miami. They like "the thrill," they tell me. They like the "music"—my quotation marks, I admit. It doesn't matter to them that the story is false or misleading propaganda. "It's only entertainment," they insist—and that's just what worries me. Why do they respond most strongly to that kind of entertainment? What do they like about it? I was stunned on entering the bedroom of one such—posters of bloody wounds, plastic/rubber "sculptures" dripping, or seeming to, with gore, skin and limbs rotting, faces in agony, silent screams of pain and despair. What I've heard of the music these folks prefer would provide the sound track for those posters. It is necrophilia.

A smoker, lamenting the fact that there is less and less space for him in restaurants and airports, exclaimed, "We're a dying breed!" But he didn't see any humor and didn't want to discuss the insight hidden in his exclamation—that his smoking was killing him and that we didn't want his second-hand smoke to kill us, too. Another smoker was willing to talk about it. "If you can assure me that I can avoid dying by quitting, I'll quit. But you can't. So don't try to force your ideas on me. I have my rights."

Necrophilia may well be a legitimate response of some "philosophers" to the fact of our mortality. "I'm going to die anyway, and so are you, and so is everybody, so what the hell difference does it make when and how?" But there's something wrong with the logic there. It amounts to saying that the Cosmos is poorly arranged, that organic forms ought not to be temporary, or at least that that person's favorite form, that is, himself, ought to continue forever. The name of that is "ego."

Perhaps exception could be taken in those extreme cases in which life is so miserable, that people have convinced themselves that they prefer death to life, really. Necrophilia can be a comment on how bad life is, for some. But if suicide is what smokers want, why do they select such a slow method, and why do they insist on involving the rest of us? And can anything be done to help people, especially while young, discover some of the joy and wonder of life, so that they don't choose death, either deliberately or by default?

I worry about the life/death orientation of the majority of our scientists and legislators and voting citizens. The percentage of scientists in military research in our nation indicates that the necrophilous orientation is in full swing among them. I talk to them about the fact that their work, their insight, their genius and their skill are all dedicated to destruction and death. "Oh, we don't think about that. It's a puzzle, presented to us, and we go about solving it. Then another puzzle presents itself and we solve that. It's exciting when we succeed. We don't think about what's at the far end."

I then tend to become a little indignant. "Well, let me tell you, it's high time and past time, that you think about what you're doing! You can't defend a nation and its supposed values by destroying it and the whole planet. You're on the verge of destroying humanity entirely. You're a threat to the Biosphere itself. If you're not stopped, and then put to work solving our real problems, you'll conclude both history and evolution. You are agents of megadeath on such a scale that you threaten the life process itself. How can you not think about it?"

"Oh, they aren't so stupid as to let that happen," the scientists assure me.

"They, *who?* Politicians are extremely stupid! And it's not a question of stupid! It's a question of necrophilia!"

"Necro-what?"

"Love of death!"

Mass murderers and gang rapists are necrophiliacs, and so are those who would hire them and then label them freedom fighters. Inventors and manufacturers and legislators who vote in favor of the manufacture and storage and possible use of nerve gas are all necrophiliacs. Humanity does not need any nerve gas, to defend anything.

I'm not the first to wonder why those who protest all this constitute such a tiny number of people. Why isn't every mother who has given the gift of life, every grandparent who sees the life process continuing in those fragile little bundles, every person who has ever been in love, every person who can see a rainbow or a sunset or a trumpet vine or a hummingbird, every person who has ever created music, ever listened to music, ever painted a painting, ever stood in awe in front of a painting, ever written a poem or a book, ever read a book and felt thoughtful afterward—why aren't we all out in the streets insisting that this necrophilia *must stop*?

Erich Fromm suspected it was because those little flashes of biophilia, love of life, which bubble up are outweighed in us by our petty daily problems of getting ahead, or getting by, or staying even—so much so that we don't feel enough of the love of life and gratitude for life to motivate ourselves to move to help preserve it.

Unamuno confronted the Fascist general who conquered the University of Salamanca in the Spanish Civil War. Unamuno called him a necrophiliac to his face, because the general's slogan and war cry was, *"¡Viva la Muerte!"* [Long live Death!] The slogan doesn't even make sense, when one tries to analyze it. How can Death live? Yet it expresses necrophilia perfectly.

Death does need to be accepted as a part of the human experience, and even welcomed, finally, I believe. But the love of death as a life-style for all the meantime, before the end of life, is a perversion.

Martin Luther King said that the victims of injustice who submitted without protest became perpetrators themselves of that injustice. Likewise, those victims of other people's necrophilia who allow ourselves and our biosphere and our planet to be swept away without protest are ourselves participating in that necrophilia.

Some live by the myth of necrophilia and they have created great and immediate danger. The rest of us need to protest! We need to join together and stop them, while we still can!

D. The Warrior

There seems to be some kind of primal inclination in humans, especially the males, to spar and compete and jostle and fight. For several thousand years there have been professional fighters. Many humans think that fighting is part of human nature and that no logic and no effort and no retraining will be able to make humans quit doing it.

Propagandists have gotten into the act, twisting the facts badly. "You are defending home and children!"

"... Free men shall stand between their loved homes and the war's desolation."

"They are 'freedom fighters'!"

All these phrases have been contaminated beyond recovery by recent prevaricators, but at last it is clear exactly what they have been doing. The name of The War Department was changed to The Department of Defense, just as it became clear to all that defense was not what was going on, but rather "imperialist aggression." Extreme sticklers for truth prefer the older name. Confucius would have. When asked what would need to be done first, if he came to power, he replied, "The rectification of names."

The militarists find unemployed young men, train them to be mass murderers, pay them and then teach them that what they are doing is a good thing. They'll use the word "patriotic," which comes from *patria* [fatherland]. *"Dulce et decorum est pro patria morire.* " [Sweet and fitting it is to die for the Fatherland.] The warrior myth is one of the most popular myths to die by that mankind has ever devised. Incalculable millions have died before their time because of it.

There are dozens of variations on the same theme. Norse warriors went to Valhalla to carouse with the gods, after being slaughtered. Japanese warriors died for the emperor and went to eternal bliss as a reward. Roman gladiators, mock warriors in the show-biz arena of their day, cried to Caesar, even when he was certifiably insane, "We who are about to die salute you!" and then they did die in desperation, merely to entertain the mob.

In our culture the warrior myth still functions, albeit in truncated form. The way of the warrior is the one approved way out of the ghetto. However, not much is said nowadays about the dead warrior. The location of his bones is important, especially if there is doubt about the justice of the cause he died in. But what's become of *him* is seldom mentioned. The injustice of his cause is not fully faced, either, perhaps out of some sort of embarrassed respect for him. He was made a fool of, by his own government, but after all, he gave his life. We weep, as we read the names on a black marble wall, but as a nation, we do not renounce the national policy which caused that needless suffering, and we do not "apologize" in any way to those who suffered vastly more deaths and maiming then we did, and all because of us.

Our national anthem is a warrior-myth song.

> Then conquer we must,
> For our cause it is just,
> And this be our motto,
> "In God is our trust."

If the second line in the above verse isn't true, then the motto sounds hollow, and persons giving their lives look foolish, at best. Yet the warrior myth persists.

Patriotism is the great idolatry of our time. General Patton told it plainly. "We're not here to die for our country. We're here to make sure the other son-of-a-bitch dies for *his* country." The game is killing, after all, not defending. Our beloved homes are not being defended, anyone can plainly see, by killing and dying in the Persian Gulf, or Central America, any more than they were in Vietnam. And what about our beloved homes in Rocky Flats, or Hanford, or Savannah River, poisoned by our own nuclear waste?

Militarism has become the new "higher power," to which our culture looks for sustenance and life. Our "jobs" depend on it. Now they've made warriors out of every last taxpayer, and with the same risk of dying for nothing, i.e., to no purpose.

In recent wars, and certainly in the pending Big and Final War, there are no "non-combatants." Millions of people uncomplainingly pay their taxes to pay for their own extinction in the Final War. They regard the warrior myth as good enough to die by. Many thoughtful people have told me they'll be heading toward Ground Zero, if any movement at all is possible during those ten minutes of warning time we're allowing ourselves. They want to die. They seek obliteration. They'd rather be zapped than melt away gradually over days and weeks in the irradiated aftermath. Meanwhile they make no effective protest about the preparation for both zapification and irradiation. They're sticking with the myth. Better dead than red, or brown, or green. Better dead than alive.

A retired Navy pilot was asked if he missed flying since returning from Vietnam. "Flying isn't fun anymore," he replied. "It's no fun unless you're dropping bombs on people." He didn't say, "Dropping bombs on people took the fun out of flying." I could have understood that. No—he said that flying wasn't fun anymore, since he was no longer dropping bombs on anyone. Notice how quickly and inevitably this warrior myth leads to mental illness, individual and collective. It *is* mental illness, and its name is necrophilia, love of death.

Where do warriors come from? Many, over the centuries, were conscripted, drafted, forced to "sign up" according to one quota system or another, medieval or modern, fair or unfair. Some were persuaded by the pay, and did it for the money. They are called "mercenaries."

Some did it out of a type of altruism, for the sake of others. When it really *is* defense, there may be something to be said for it. Marathon, Thermopylae, Little Big Horn and Dien Bien Phu come to mind, when the defenders won and it made a difference. Everything depends on which side one is referring to. One thing for certain, the word "defense" is used incorrectly and ungrammatically in current North American culture, as in phrases like, "the defense budget."

Many warriors became such because of the warrior myth. They believe in what they are doing. Also their "training" includes believing in it. They will obey commands because they are commands, regardless of logic, necessity, justice, legality or even the so-called instinct of self-preservation. They have an esprit de corps which overrides that instinct. Once combat begins and comrades begin to fall, it becomes revenge for downed buddies. Politics, geopolitics, ideology and reason count for little on the battlefield. After the battle, however, a myth is needed to justify what happened and what was done. When that myth fails, or is lacking, serious trouble results for the warrior-cause itself.

That's what happened in Vietnam. The "peacenik" protestors did not end that war, in the name of peace and human solidarity and moral rectitude. The Vietnam Veterans against the War ended that war. They were the sure sign that the warrior myth had failed. They threw their Purple Heart medals into bonfires, and such symbolic acts pulled the rug out from under the politicians and military strategists.

"Our country is grateful to the fallen warrior."

"The fallen warrior has made life better for those he left behind."

"Their honor and courage will never be forgotten."

"My only regret is that I have but one life to give for my country."

"We're still looking for a few good men."

"Be all that you can be."

These are some of the phrases which express that myth. But you can be more than a killer robot which obeys orders unthinkingly. And all the fallen warriors of history have not solved any of mankind's problems.

Warriors nowadays return from combat with syndromes of symptoms that refer to stress and trauma and subsequent "disorder," because the myth used to justify what they did is faulty, unconvincing, patently false, and everyone knows it.

Ernest Hemingway "leaked" the truth of it. "They wrote in the old days that it is sweet and fitting to die for one's country. But in modern war there is nothing sweet nor fitting in your dying. You will die like a dog for no good reason."

C. S. Lewis was generally quite a careful thinker, but he erred with regard to the warrior myth. He claimed that war itself could not be condemned, because it brought out the best in humans—courage, brave deeds and cooperation. But hurricanes and volcanos can do the same thing, without the infusion of the guilt of knowing that all the destruction and all the dead people are our own doing. And besides that, war has changed. There is not much worthwhile camaraderie, not much respect for the enemy. It is more and more mechanized, waged by mercenaries, designed to influence fat budgets at home. War itself can be, and must finally be, condemned and repudiated, after all.

The warrior myth is moribund, but does not die. It seems clear that this myth is unworthy of our allegiance. The words of many a Vietnam veteran state it plainly: "I'll never believe my government again." And it's worse now than it was then—now that we have Disinformation Departments, "plausible deniability," an announced policy of pre-emptive war, and blatantly false attempts to justify invasions.

Older veterans may continue to mouth the patriotic explanations of their earlier battlefield behavior, but most of them seem a little sanguine about it. The enemy nation which they fought so bitterly sixty years ago is now the "ally." The ally back then became the supposed enemy for almost fifty years, but has now collapsed. "Don't trust him!" one can hear, but everyone *is* trusting him, except the necrophiliacs.

"We have done you warriors a great disservice," one of the last Soviet diplomats said at Geneva. "We have taken away your enemy." It has all changed, and yet nothing has changed. There was no peace dividend in the budget and no let-up in opportunities to test the latest weaponry. But maybe something is changing.

Pre-emptive war has turned into guerrilla warfare, in which the invaders are at every disadvantage. We did this once in the jungle; now our nineteen-year-olds have to do it again in the desert. But they are not gung-ho warriors. You can see it in their faces. They want to go home, which is exactly what their enemy wants them to do.

In spite of all official efforts to prevent it, news and even pictures of this horror reach home. And the next batch of cannon-fodder is becoming reluctant. There is no organized protest that we know of, but there is a growing mood. The warrior myth has lost its appeal. Only those who really like mayhem are left—the rest of us, who may yet become the majority, have grown beyond that. The glory is gone, and the money isn't worth it. "When you're dead, you're dead."

Good sense may be setting in. "Do I really want to get killed or maimed for nothing? Is it worth it, just for oil and oil profits?"

કોકોકો

VIII

STORIES FROM PRACTICAL OBSERVATION

In our survey of the stories, beliefs and metaphors that we use to try to deal with Death it is time to consider the observable, the obvious and the unavoidable. Untestable speculations will become too tempting to resist later, but first we need to consider what is perfectly clear. What can we perceive personally and directly, and what shall we make of that?

Thomas Carlisle was told that Lady Whatsername, who was something of an amateur philosopher, "had decided to accept the Universe." His gruff retort was, "By God, she'd better!" What kind of Universe is this? And let's leave "God," as in Carlisle's expletive, out of it for now.

Dr. Beverly Kunkle, teaching biology and anatomy at Lafayette College more than fifty years ago, introduced me to the philosophical implications of scientific observation. "Any lover of Truth will be willing to follow Truth wherever that trail leads." His words have given me courage many times, and have convinced me that no myth that ignores truth is worthy of allegiance.

≥●

A. The Machine Stops

A nephew came visiting recently, wearing an all black T-shirt with delicate white lettering:

LIFE IS HARD
AND THEN YOU DIE.

We greeted him and his charming, vivacious wife, chuckling grimly at the message on his shirt, and then went on to enjoy each other, and to prove, for one evening at least, that the T-shirt message wasn't so. Life is full and exciting and enjoyable, at least some of the time. But then, you die. That fact still stands, inexorable.

Many thoughtful people, who have done with myths and fairy tales, dismissing them all as childish and unrealistic, consider the metaphor of the machine their own. A human being is his body. The body is a machine, marvelous and complex. And, like all machines, it wears out at last. One may as well face the fact, although it doesn't really matter whether you accept it or not. The machine wears out, and stops.

This looks quite realistic. It regards the body as a mechanical device rather than an organism, however, and they are not quite the same. An organism can and does replace itself, over and over—all new cells every seven years in our case—so why does it need to wear out?

Some years ago a group within the so-called New Age Movement called themselves the Immortalists. They were picking up on the medieval myth of the alchemist, the true master of pure occult power. Part of the achievement of a true Adept included such control of his body that Death was overcome. Part of the lore includes stories of extremely old Magicians, not prestidigitators—several centuries old, that is, not one hundred twenty years. The claim is that they are persons who channel and embody Cosmic Power, and therefore do not die.

The Immortalists implied that they were such persons also, and tried to enlist others into a larger movement, by insisting that dying was a culturally controlled and even culturally caused event. We become old and die because our culture teaches us that we must, they said. I must admit to being intrigued by this idea. Our culture is, to be sure, very hard on our bodies.

Our culture taught us to smoke when we were young, for example. It teaches us to acquiesce in the ingestion and breathing of large quantities of poison. It provides stress in quantities sufficient to break down our immune systems. It pays some of us to prepare extremely deadly materials in huge quantities and then it calls that "defense." It fills our heads with violent stories and calls that entertainment. It is possible for me to imagine that persons who found ways to reject this cultural input, this toxic life-style, could live longer, maybe quite a bit longer.

Could the immortalists be right in their claim that we die only because our culture teaches us that we must and we allow it? Can the body clock, which governs aging, the rate of aging, and ultimately death itself, be reset? But the clock is a metaphor. No one has located it, no one knows how it really works, and no one has yet succeeded in taking charge of it.

The myth of the machine that stops is tied to the law of entropy. Everything winds down. Everything is part of a machine which is stopping. The end of all processes is random motion, which is chaos, which seems to be equivalent to Nothing and is called the Void in many myths.

I suspect that the Second Law of Thermodynamics, from which this entropy concept is derived, has been overstated by some, as if it were a philosophical beacon. If the most probable state of matter is pure amorphous undifferentiated Chaos, which is what the "law" says, why is there a Cosmos at all? On the contrary, the Cosmos is all Order, and all *in order*.

"Maybe so," whimper the advocates of entropy, "but it all

ends in Chaos. It all dies and decays."

They're whining about change. They themselves end in dissolution. But it is an overstatement to claim that The Whole Thing changes from Order to Chaos. It changes from one kind of order to another. And they still haven't explained where all the order came from in the first place. And now some, studying turbulence in air and water, have discovered the Laws of Chaos, which sounds like even more Order!

Entropy doesn't account for where Order comes from, and the Order we have includes organisms and the regeneration of organisms and the reproduction of organisms. The Void is the Source of all manifest Order, somehow.

Even the not-much-feared but certainly possible Thermonuclear Destruction of the Biosphere on the Third Planet out from Helios will not be Disorder, not pure amorphous Chaos. It will entail blast, radiation, heat and cold, producing conditions in which our kind of life cannot predictably survive, to be sure. That's the reason why we should prevent it, if we can, if there's still time. But it still will be another type of Order. It will still be the Cosmos.

It'll be that part of the Cosmos in which intelligence, so-called, destroyed itself. But we have no business blaming that on entropy, thus excusing those who want to destroy what we're so fond of, that is, this Live Planet, by saying that it is all inevitable anyway, as if what they're destroying was doomed anyway, so what the hell...

Belief in Entropy could be used as our human psychological equivalent to traumatized animals going into shock. Here comes the end. So, I'll just turn my mind off, and my body, from here inside, and be extinguished.

The Immortalists deny all this. The problem with their denial of the ultimate stoppage of the machine is that there is no known case of any exception to the observation that all bodies wear out and die. That is, there is no known case that isn't a myth. So, the most sensible thing is to suppose that one's own body will do likewise. Whether that is the same as annihilation depends partly on whether a human being really is nothing more than the physical body.

Annihilation can be made to look quite attractive. Wouldn't oblivion be better than the hell of eternal conscious torment found in the sadistic teachings of the Medieval Church and the modern fundamentalists?

The Preacher in Ecclesiastes said it was better to be a live dog than a dead lion. W. C. Fields wanted it stated on his tombstone that he'd rather be in Philadelphia, and he didn't like Philadelphia much. Achilles said he'd rather be a slave on earth than a king in the realm of dead phantoms. We can't be sure about The Preacher and W. C. Fields, but Achilles is comparing being alive to being dead and *not* annihilated. When one compares being alive to being blotto, it depends on what life was like, or promises to be like from here to the end. In some circumstances death can be called "deliverance," even if it is annihilation.

Epicurus said death was the deprivation of sensation, and believed that the "soul" did not survive death any more than the body did. The atoms, of both, disperse at death, he said. "Death, the most terrifying of all ills [as some think] is nothing to us, since as long as we exist, death is not with us, and when death comes, then we do not exist."

"I don't care where I'm buried."

"Dispose of the remains as inexpensively as possible, with no fuss."

"I don't care who comes to my funeral."

"I don't want any funeral or memorial service at all."

Different individuals have said all of the above to me. They do not believe that they will be around in any sense at all after death. "I don't care what people say. I won't be caring what the neighbors think. It won't bother me."

The machine stops. Modern philosophers like Freud and Schopenhauer and Heidegger, as well as Ernest Becker in **The**

Denial of Death, referred to earlier, have observed that deep down contemporary man does not really believe in his own death. "All men are mortal, but not I. All men will die, except me."

The realists, who do believe that the machine really does stop, remind us of Death's inevitability and also of Death's finality. Many of the myths of mankind deny one or the other of these two things.

The Machine Stops. Medical science and advanced meditation techniques can keep it going longer, but then it stops. There are no known exceptions. Stories persist that Yogis and Adepts live to be very old, some of them. There are very old people living in the Caucasus Mountains. But there are none who do not die eventually.

In the meantime the machine can be better taken care of. Smoking really is stupid. We already know of the value of exercise. We used to call it work. Injury and abuse will demand payback, sooner or later. Consider the current condition of many retired boxers. If it's a machine, and the process is mechanical, then for every action there is an equal and opposite reaction.

I recall my high school biology teacher lamenting my inordinate desire to play football, given my size and poor eyesight. Neither he nor I quite understood that it was my adolescent need to prove virility and enhance ego that made me want to play so very much. He warned that all the hits, all the blows, all the falls and bruises would take their toll—that the machine was made for a pre-determined quantity of use or punishment only, and that it was foolish to subject it to so much meaningless and needless abuse while it was young and still maturing. The arthritis in my elbow and shoulder now causes me to suspect that he was right.

If it is all mechanism, then the brain/mind/logic/reason function is part of it. Everybody's machine includes this ability, even though not everybody uses it much. The human group has multiplied and collected the products of this function and calls that Knowledge/Science, and from that sector we can hear a clear word. Several clear words, in fact.

[1] Your ego, and your body, are not an exception. You may as well begin to deal with that fact now. Some people refuse to make their last will and testament, and refuse to think about plans for their own funeral and burial. That's superstition, as if thinking about it will cause it. It's nonsense.

[2] Take care of your machine. No smoking. Be useful. Work. Play. Exercise. Eat and drink correctly.

[3] Be gentle with other machines. They're only trying to get through this maze, just as you are. If life's a bitch, as I've heard tell, if life is hard and then you die, then when Death and Fairness and Irony and Poetic Justice come up for conversation, be thoughtful of the other person. Maybe, being loving and gentle, we can get through this. No whimpering. Let's see your courage. We're all in this together, and nobody gets out of here alive. Life is a fatal disease.

A dear friend, a realist and a lover of people and of life, confides to me that he thinks Blotto is the belief he's best reconciled to, in the life-after-death question. You're dead, and when you're dead, you're dead. It's all over, when it's over. He quotes Shakespeare to me: "*The coward dies a thousand deaths, the valiant do die but once.*" Then he adds, "But Death is what makes living precious. Death is what creates Now. Otherwise it would be 'forever' already! We'd be always putting it off, whatever. Death reminds you not to put it off. Do it, if you're going to."

This feels a little harsh, but it makes sense. It fits the evidence we have. Something in me whispers that surely there's more to it than that, but that may be weakness and whistling in the void, on my part.

٨

B. Sundown

"Day is dying in the west," we used to sing at vespers. Sundown has become a symbol. The dying of the day, the pending end of the interval of daylight we have just had, can be taken as a metaphor for our own dying, also.

The word "sunset" is already a metaphor before we add dying to the mixture. We now know, thanks to mathematicians and careful observers, that the sun is not setting at all. With reference to the earth the sun is not moving. The earth is spinning on its axis, and "sundown" is our word for the fact that the spot on the surface of the earth where we are is about to move out of sight of the sun which blazes away at all times. This portion of the daily spin, when we were receiving light from the sun, is about to end and we're heading into the dark portion when we won't be facing the sun.

Standing or sitting here on the surface of the earth, this "correction" of what we can observe still seems somewhat remarkable and even farfetched. It sure looks like the sun is going down, closer and closer to the horizon, and then on down behind it.

Traveling by air, in the vicinity of the north pole in November, helped me really see the truth of it. The pink ice floe beneath us was fascinating, but even more remarkable was the way our movements caused the sun to set and then reappear and then set again!

In spite of all that, the metaphor still stands as a reference to our own mortality. Sundown is a tiny crisis in the cycle of light/dark/light/dark. It can become a symbol of that other crisis, that stage of life which we are all drifting into. "He's in the sunset of his life."

The time of day is the symbol. We also have songs that use the time of year to symbolize the same thing.

"Oh, it's a long, long time, from May to December...
November! December!"

I was noting this with an older couple. "It feels like I'm in
maybe late October," I said. The older gentleman, who was not
at all well, exclaimed, "Some of us are at December thirtieth!"
And he was.

What time is it? Does it matter, as much as it used to? We
can tell we are near the end, right? Time for thinking,
remembering, reviewing, perhaps evaluating.

Sometimes we notice the beauty of the sunset. The ordinary
is cast in a new light. Wavelengths of reflected light on clouds
and treetops and mountains catch our attention. The colors are
not ordinary. We think about light in a new light.

"Let there be light!"

"More light! More light!" exclaimed Goethe at his last
moment.

If life is light, and death is darkness, then death is the other
half of the whole process. Yin and Yang go together to make up
the whole.

We as a culture don't sit and watch sunsets as much as we
used to. We're distracted by the evening "news," what some call,
"the daily negative prayer." These are the things that we hoped
wouldn't happen this day, but did. The fretting that goes with
getting and spending preoccupies us. But sometimes sundown
insists that we pay attention. Besides the beauty, it calls us to
calmness, and realism, and peace.

A student brought to class a children's story she had written.
The heart of it was an animated paper bag, the main character in
the story, who went around announcing, "I'm biodegradable!"
The class wasn't sure the story worked, or would work for
children, but it struck me very hard, as a possible story for people
in the sunset of their lives.

"We're biodegradable!" Maybe we should wear a badge, or
a tattoo in the middle of our foreheads which announces, "I'm
biodegradable!" We get away with forgetting that for moments

at a time, but maybe if we saw that tattoo on the next person, it would remind us. I'm biodegradable, and it's getting late.

C. Rest for the Weary

Tombstones used to display the initials R.I.P., which in either Latin or English mean, "Rest in Peace," expressing the wish of the survivors for the dearly departed.

The neighbors' dog kept me awake at night for three years. Sleep, undisturbed sleep, came to feel very good on the rare occasions when it was allowed. If a good night's sleep feels so delicious, can being dead really be so very bad? The thought crossed my mind.

Dysentery has made being alive for me so utterly miserable, at times, that I have described the feeling, only slightly exaggerated, "I was afraid I might not die!" The reason we get sick, one could say, is to teach us to accept being dead. It'll be a relief to be excused from all this misery, one thinks. Why would anyone want to fight Death? What kind of myth would it take to be strong enough to override the logic and the desire for relief that Death will bring!

Sleep is the cure for illness. When the sick person falls asleep, the watchers know he is on the mend. But if that's so, then it's no wonder it has occurred to people to ask whether Death may not be the real, final cure.

Suicide is a way out of an unbearable situation. In an old TV western, prisoners who had been made into mining slaves attempted to escape. One was shot—a bull's eye in the target which was part of the prison uniform. Another prisoner muttered over his companion's dead body, "Found a way out."

Sigmund Freud woke up from a fainting spell, after a verbal conflict with Carl Jung, and murmured, "How sweet it must be to die." He believed Death meant oblivion, yet he could say that laying down the burden of responsibility and conflict and authority could be sweet, that the yielding and relief could be "worth it."

Death is seen as an escape, and sleep is the symbol of it, which we experience every night of our lives. When we are deprived of sleep, we long for death.

What is the difference between going to sleep, and dying? When I go to sleep, I let go of consciousness. It is an act of trust. I let the Cosmos, or that symbol of the Cosmos, "God," look after me, while my attention is absent. Without that kind of trust, sleep is difficult, and dying is more difficult than it would need to be, if I can tell by observation.

Pandit Usharbudh Arya, in his book, **Meditation and the Art of Dying**, from the Himalayan International Institute of Yoga Science and Philosophy, states:

> Willingly or unwillingly, with contentment or with resentment, an insomniac finally falls asleep. One dies in the same manner. Not being able to sleep easily is a disease. Not being able to die easily is also a disease. Dying is no disease; only not being able to die is the disease. Hanging on there, not wanting to go, clutching the external awareness, not wanting to sleep, a hidden part of the person keeping him awake when he should be asleep, keeping him here when he should be gone—we must recognize this disease of not being able to die happily.

Children don't like being put to bed too early, and often resist sleep, even though they're exhausted. Every parent has observed this. My memory of being the child "who had to go to bed by day" was that I wasn't finished with the day yet. I wanted to do more, see more, listen to more stories, learn more, play more. How dare they go on doing things when I'm not here?

For us adults a loss of interest in the world, in current events, in little kids, in newness generally, may be a signal of the approach of Death. "Life's not that interesting anymore."

When I go to sleep, I let go of consciousness, but I do expect to wake up again. Yet, as I get older, I find it more and more of a surprise, when I awaken in the morning. "Oh! You're back. Back here! And I'm me again." Often I am aware of having been someone else and somewhere else, in dreams. The process of waking up fills me with wonder.

My father was afraid to fall asleep in his last days. It was, perhaps, too much like dying. He told me he was afraid of the dreams that came in sleep. The dreams reminded him, warned him, perhaps, and foreshadowed for him that Great Encounter which he feared after Death.

My mother, in contrast, was not permitted to sleep, in her last days. It must have turned into torture. The lights were kept on day and night, at my father's insistence. No sleep. No rest. She was disturbed, in order to wait on him, every two minutes, literally, all the day and all the night. When she sat on that stool after breakfast that last day, she must have been asking for rest. A break in the action. Time out. Annihilation, even, if that's what's pending, would come as sweetly as sleep to the weary, the utterly weary. And when you are tired enough, dreams do not disturb your rest. There was not enough violence in her departure to knock her off that stool.

Florida Scott-Maxwell wrote in her remarkable book, **The Measure of My Days**: "I do not know what I believe about life after death; if it exists, then I burn with interest; if not—well, I am weary."

Older people report to me that at times they are wakeful in the night, sometimes awakened by an unpleasant dream, and feel filled with a strange unaccountable Dread. What is this? Dread of what? Worry isn't quite the right word for it.

Sometimes the worries which I refuse to indulge in during the day disturb me at night, but this Dread seems to be something else. I have felt it. In some dreams, fear awakens the sleeper, but there is little to be afraid of, not even very much to worry about.

After breakfast and T'ai Ch'ih exercises they fly forgotten. But I have sensed that Dread, nevertheless.

Persons whose lives are filled with psychic pain, for themselves and their loved ones, have told me that they hope there is no survival after death. They want "peace," by which they seem to mean undisturbed annihilation—blotto. They fear having to go through all this agony and misery again. They have had enough. It almost sounds Hindu, where the goal is to escape the endless round of rebirths into this life of toil and tears, to find Nirvana, absorption into the void. They're not sure that sleep is a good metaphor for Death, because sleep does include both dreams and waking up again.

I must say it makes me sad that life has been so miserable for some people that they end up with that evaluation of it. I have been spared the worst kinds of suffering, and I seem to have a high threshold for physical pain—so my personal evaluation of life is different. I want more of it, and my hope concerning Death is that it will be as good as life was.

Some people die of a broken heart. Some disappointment, some failure, some disaster, some separation, some shame—it can cause the body to shut down. Death, then, better than sleep, offers escape and rest. The body, when injured, goes into shock, and as Death nears, pain is overcome. It can happen. It can definitely account for the fact of dying in some cases, but it does not seem to be something to depend on. It is despair. It is rejection of the fact that one is alive. Is there any way we can protect the heart from breaking? We make progress in the physical aspects of that question, but the figurative meaning is so far out, the question strikes us as strange.

To fall asleep, one must let go of consciousness. Dying includes letting go of consciousness, ego, possessions, position, reputation—all that. Some philosophies of life recommend practice in advance in such giving up, or getting rid. You really can't take it with you. But if possessions and ego are stuck in your heart, in your Heart's Desire, they may foul up the process of getting you on your way.

Some old people practice "getting rid," and some do not. There was an order of monks which spent years carving their own coffins. That used to seem morbid to me, a way of not fully living. But clinging to those things which can't be taken along is likewise pretty clearly not a good idea.

A scene from early childhood comes to mind. The child must leave most of his toys there on the floor and go to bed. Maybe he can take one favorite stuffed animal. When confronting Death one can't take anything, except one's Self. That Self is what requires attention, before that last stage is reached. Raymond Moody made a careful study of near-death experiences. He has defined a little more specifically those qualities of the Self which can be taken into those experiences. He calls them "wisdom" and "skill in loving." Possessions and "achievements" don't seem to count. It also appears that this is not something one can practice in a safe place beforehand. One has to get it right the first time.

D. Making Room

Stories tell of elderly and infirm Eskimos who willingly went out on the ice floe, never to return, when their usefulness to the group was ended. **Top of the World**, by Hans Ruesch, describes the willingness of the old grandmother to go, shortly after the birth of the baby, and the willingness of the others to let her go, knowing that the new mouth to feed would replace the one leaving. The author includes a nice twist, however. The new parents go chasing after Grandma in the snow, to tell her the alarming news that the newborn baby has no teeth! Grandma seems able to handle that news, and assures them that teeth will grow. They bring her back, putting her in charge of that magic project, putting off for a while that fateful day when she will have to leave the group.

In the Japanese film, **The Ballad of Narayama**, another grandmother knocks her own teeth out, smashing her face against the stone rim of the well, in order to qualify herself as decrepit enough to be taken across the steep valley to the magic mountains where she's to be left amid the bones and the crows. She is aware that marriage and the birth of a new one have already added to the number of the group. This subservience of the individual to the group strikes us as remarkable, but it could be that our emphasis on individualism is the peculiar stance.

Stories like this sound strange to us because they are based on a loyalty to the group which we don't have. The group constitutes the individual's reason for being, among them, but not among us. Our group is too large, our families no longer that cohesive. When we see that kind of group loyalty, we are a little suspicious of pathology, as for instance in a military unit or a terrorist cell. Those individuals appear mindless and dangerous because of what they have been trained to do without question for the group.

In the end each individual must die, but the group can survive a very great deal of that. The group lives on. The group overcomes Death. The individual does not, and does not need to. The analogy of cells in our body may make it clear. We replace every cell every seven years, yet we go on, claiming to be the same person throughout, feeling like we really are the same person who fell out of the apple tree sixty years ago, eight bodies ago, and broke an arm. It depends on where the emphasis is focused. We focus ours on the individual, but it need not be done that way.

We don't have as much practice as others have had at saying to ourselves, "I am in the way. I have become a hindrance. I no longer contribute. So it's time for me to get out of the way."

Of course, persons who have never contributed anything, who have never served anyone else, who have always been members of that portion of the group that demanded to be served—they won't notice that circumstances have changed as they approach the end. Perhaps there's not much to be said that would be helpful for such persons. But those of us who have served and worked and carried our share and someone else's, too, will notice when the arrangement of things shifts.

What's your ministry? What do you have to contribute—for the good of the group, for the good of family or neighbors or humanity? "They also serve who only stand and wait," I know—up to a point. One thing for sure, all this bears serious consideration before the last minute.

An elderly person, even an infirm one, can have a ministry. Stories to tell, a smile of thanks, a perspective enlarged by time which can go by the name of wisdom and can be shared—tell it to the grandchildren. Write it down. When pain and impatience and weakness and contrariness make that sharing of the wisdom impossible, then the thing has shifted.

Then it isn't necessary to spend the family's last dime on magnificent razzle-dazzle medical marvels, or on nursing home care to keep alive someone who is in effect already gone. That is, it isn't unavoidably necessary, for instance, in other cultures. Before it comes to that point, they're able to remove themselves. They're willing to make room.

Governor Lamm of Colorado found himself in a peck of trouble some time ago for saying in public something like what I'm trying to state here. I don't think he meant what he said as a threat to anyone, and I certainly don't either. I'm not saying to those older than I, "Why don't you and your kind just get out of the way? Make room!" I'm saying, to me and my generation, "Do you suppose the day could come when I'll need the courage to be able to say to myself, 'I'm in the way! I need to make room for those whose lives aren't yet concluded'?" I'm saying, to me and my generation, "Live fully now, and begin now to muster the wherewithal to be fully responsible for our own individual departure, when the time comes."

I do think that we as a culture need to rethink this matter, and there's no time like the present. Now is the accepted time, to

start to begin to commence to initiate the process of bringing this
out into the open air.

E. Letting Go

Many observers, especially lately, are noticing that we prepare
for our individual death in the way we live. When we get old we
turn into what we've been all along, only more so, with less
pretense. And when it's time to confront Death, we'll do it in
much the same way that we've been confronting Life.

Some cower and cringe, "afraid of living and scared of
dying." They have been hurt too much, let down too often,
betrayed, perhaps. Life is full of stings and nettles, and some
haven't learned the trick of grabbing briskly to minimize the pain.
Life has become a running sore, a throbbing toothache, with no
relief.

Those who have this view of life may not see Death as a
welcome way out, but simply a door leading to more
unimaginable trouble. This may be one's habitual way of thinking
which could be changed with effort, since habits can, with effort,
be changed. Or it may be an entrenched unchangeable
philosophy of life, learned early and confirmed since. If so, it's
a tragedy. We need to spend more effort in order to arrange
things so the children of our planet do not live in such misery
that they end up with this fearful view of life.

Other people take life as it comes, passively, not daring to
expect too much, not getting their hopes up too much, for fear of
"jinxing" the process. They dare less and lose less and perhaps
suffer less, but they also miss out on much of the fun and
adventure of life. These are the people who take a "ho-hum"
attitude toward all this mythology business, suspecting that it
doesn't have to do with anything, assuming that it can't make
much difference. Since we all go down the drain in the end
anyway, why get all lathered up about it?

Then there are those others who go out to meet life, eagerly and expectantly. C. S. Lewis created such a character in his Narnia series—Reepeecheep, the Gallant Mouse, a kind of D'Artagnan character, full of wild and crazy ideas about honor. In spite of that, he had an admirable attitude toward Life, and Death. Near the beginning of each day he challenged the others around him to sally forth, "and let us see what adventure Aslan has in store for us today!" He wasn't going to cringe, and he wasn't going to just sit there passively. He was on his way to meet whatever was coming.

I'm suggesting that exactly this attitude can be one's myth to live and die by. Go to meet whatever mystery lies behind that door. Go through, go on through. Let go of this stage, which is over, and on to the next, whatever it is. My father stalled in the middle of the process of dying. He announced that it was hard to let go, and he would not.

I can't help thinking of a story that circulated among us young preachers ages ago—we didn't dare use it in any of our sermons because of the last word, which remains until now quite untranslatable into "proper" pulpit language. A man fell off a cliff but on his way down grabbed a juniper root that was jutting out into thin air, and there he dangled. He prayed, "Oh, God! Save me! Save me!"

A voice answered him, "I will save you, but you must obey."

"Oh, is that you, Lord? Oh, yes! Anything! Save me. I'll do anything!"

"Very well. Here's the first thing you must do."

"What? What? Yes, Lord! Save me!"

"Let go."

The man looked around, and down, and wiggled his legs a little. Finally he called out, *"Bullshit!"*

I guess I was expecting my father to let go willingly and deliberately, considering his professed beliefs and the stage he was at and the condition he was in and the unpleasant consequences caused already by his hanging on so. However, as

I think about it now after some time has passed, I realize that he never was a Reepeecheep type of person. He took life passively, at best. Late in the game, I wrote to him, giving him permission to go on, to let go, just in case that was the problem, but he gave the clear impression that he didn't appreciate the gesture.

Now I wonder, was I acting the part of Job's wife, who told him in the midst of his sufferings, "Curse God and die"? I don't think so, but maybe. Life—especially that long drawn-out part of it near the end, for some, thanks to modern medical science—can be thought of as something to curse and be glad to be rid of. But I don't think that was what I was recommending.

I was trying to say to him, using his own mythology, "Trust God and die." Let's let "God" mean The Whole Thing. Trust it, and die. Let go. You have to, anyway. Why fight it? And why delay any more?

When news came that my father had died in the nursing home, nine days after we put him there the afternoon of our mother's funeral, I wondered what happened as he died. How did my father go? No one knows. They found him dead at 5:30 in the morning. I for certain do not know with what attitude or mood he went.

I'd like to be able to believe that he finally did let go deliberately and that he knew a moment of surrender, of peace, even of triumph, as he did it.

As children we knew a challenge which comes to mind now. A skinny kid could crawl down inside the girders of The Bridge in our town, that same town, and wriggle down onto the top of the concrete pier that stood in the middle of the creek. Adults and fat kids could not do it. I remember the first day I did it. It was quite an achievement, not because I wasn't skinny enough, but because there was only one way off the top of that pier.

Jump. Jump into the rushing waters of Loyalsock Creek and be swept away to the stony beach yonder. Other kids did it. They did it all the time. No kid who had ever gotten onto that pier had ever not jumped off. You see the analogy. I sat a long time, hugging myself with my long skinny arms, shivering with cold and a kind of dread. I sat a long time, and then suddenly, like a hop-toad, I sprang out and was there in mid-air, dropping, plunging into the water, touching bottom with my toes, wishing I had taken in a little more air—

Did Dad jump? Or did they have to drag him off? I don't know. For his sake I hope he jumped.

૪ૂૐ૪ૐ

IX

STORIES FROM RELIGION, WHICH PRESERVE EGO

"Ego" is the Latin word for "I"—the first person singular personal pronoun. It is what most of us unthinkingly consider first. First person. "I think, therefore I am." "I think I think, therefore I think I am."

In his study of the human mind, Freud described the Ego and the Id. The Id is the source of instinct and desire. The Ego is the thinking, managing part, the part that has to adapt to the world and the culture and the rules. Often the desires of the Id amount to a sort of harassment of the Ego, which has to make arrangements and adaptations and compromises and rationalizations in order to get, or try to get, what the Id wants.

The Ego is a function of the brain. It will not function after the brain dies. The ego is a fiction, a convention, a metaphor, an invention constructed by the brain to help the brain preserve itself. Alan Watts wrote a marvelous little book, entitled **The Book**, in which he demonstrates that the Ego isn't really there at all. His subtitle was **On the Secret of Knowing Who You Really Are**. I highly recommend it.

The Ego is a survival device. Its function is to preserve itself, and the brain and the organism that invented it. It can be very useful in the task of self-preservation, using memory and inference and imagination to preserve the individual organism. "The last time wolves chased me, it helped to climb a tree." "This interview will be more successful if I smile." The ego's sole function is self-preservation. The ego can hardly imagine its own death. Death is an unmanageable problem, for ego.

In a culture so committed to individualism, achievement and celebrity-worship, ego can cause much trouble, even before death looms and demands attention. "I'm not measuring up." "I'm a failure." "I'm growing old, weakening." "I feel rejected and lonely." Death lies in wait as the final insult. Ego suffers greatly, watching its own pending demise approach inexorably.

As we continue our survey of beliefs, stories and metaphors that deal with dying, we find two more groups of stories. I call one group "religion," and note how these stories attempt to preserve ego. They comfort and strengthen ego, by lying to it, saying, "You can survive." "You shall not die." Religions say to ego, "Submit—to rules and/or hierarchical authority—and you will avoid the consequences of organic existence, which include the annihilation of every individual organism."

The final group of stories I call "philosophy," the love of wisdom, because in one way or another, they help us move beyond that bondage to ego. Some may find this a new and bizarre use of the terms "religion" and "philosophy," but I believe the evidence bears out this usage.

A. Only My Group Has the Truth

Nationalism is the belief that one's own country is the best and has some kind of right to order other nations around. We have already looked at it, because of its world-wide prevalence. Until just lately it has been a root cause of almost all modern warfare.

Ethnocentrism is similar, but is centered on the ethnic group, on race, or language, or ancient shared customs. Some modern nations, like Spain, Canada, the U.S.S.R. and Yugoslavia, have had a hard time holding themselves together because of ethnocentrism. The underlying message is, "The group that I'm a member of is the best, and our language and our customs are correct and need to be preserved and expanded at all costs."

Some forms of ethnocentrism are comical, after they are pointed out. "My God, they drive on the wrong side of the road!" "Why don't they eat correctly, instead of using chopsticks?" "What're all these pesetas worth in *real* money," the loud-mouthed tourist asks the waitress. Sometimes it isn't very funny. Ethnocentric people should stay home.

A special form of this self-centered attitude, applied to one's own group, could be called, "creedism," or, "creedalism." "Only my group has the truth, and we have all of it." It is the arrogance of those who really know. "We are right, they are wrong. They live in error, in darkness. They are deceived and deceiving. We have the truth, the Whole Unchangeable Truth that will not shift with time nor with widened or altered perspective. Those benighted persons do not know the truth and need for us to tell it to them. They are lost. If they don't believe us, after we tell them the Truth, then they are doubly lost."

This group is held together by the common belief system, that is, by whatever myth all the members are required to adhere to. Members who stop believing, for whatever reason, are cast into outer darkness. Open-minded persons are despised, as unbelievers and bad examples and bad teachers.

I used to belong to such a group and I can recall the treatment I received as my perspective widened and changed. I came to realize that the little creed I had been taught did not contain all truth, that I didn't know everything, that, in fact, I knew very little. Finally I reached the point where I was sure of only one thing, namely that I didn't know very much at all. It was extremely liberating to find a teacher, and then later to become the same kind of teacher, who could exclaim, "Gosh! It beats me! I don't know! Let's check it out. What do *you* think? What do you know about it?"

Many live by the myth that only their group has the truth. We could ignore them, because the notion is ridiculous, but they are very powerful and dangerous and their simple-minded answers appeal to the frustrated, the fearful and the angry. They are called Fundamentalists, in all the major religions. They believe that their doctrines are "fundamental."

Fundamentalist Jews are extreme right-wing orthodox practitioners, formerly led in Israel by Rabbi Meir Kahane. They are utterly uncompromising toward the Palestinians, ready to exterminate them, believing that God made them to be slaves and that therefore they have no right to object or resist. At the same time these people are totally unbending toward all other Jews, who may refuse or fail to adhere in some way to the strictest interpretation of traditional Jewish taboos. They even deny that these others really are Jews at all, much to the consternation of those who are providing most of the funding, one way or another, for the Zionist State of Israel.

Fundamentalist Muslims were represented by the late Ayatollah of Iran. The Afghan Mujahadeen, to whom Americans loved to give extremely deadly weapons, were even more conservative and more dangerous than he ever was. They became the Taliban. These fundamentalists leave a bloody trail wherever they go, because they believe that they are right and all the rest of the world is wrong, and they are ready to die for that belief. They have become a threat to the only surviving super-power, and that threat in turn has put the traditional rights and liberties of the citizens of that power at risk.

Fundamentalist Roman Catholics are represented by the previous Pope of Rome, John Paul II, his successor, Benedict XVI, his Curia, and his Fascist supporters all over the world. Opus Dei is a well-known and powerful support group. Murder and deception are commonly used weapons; one of the more notable examples is the elimination by murder of the previous Pontiff's predecessor, John Paul I. See **In God's Name**, by David Yallop.

The reforms of Pope John XXIII are being rejected and undone and it is full steam astern, back to the High Middle Ages, in theology and in political arrangements. Outside the Pope's jurisdiction there is no salvation, he says, and only he is right.

There will be no compromise with women or with Liberation Theology. He has been quick to ally himself with Fascist Death-squad dictators. When they murdered liberal bishops, as in El Salvador, the Vatican did not object.

Fundamentalist Protestants have had much publicity lately, not all of it good. Scandals involving TV evangelists have tarnished their reputation somewhat, although less than one would logically expect or hope. Ethical behavior has never been a long suit among them, partly because membership in their group does not depend on behavior but upon professed belief. Dishonest persons can always do well, just by saying, "I believe," whether it's true or not.

One of their number, Oliver North, became famous two decades ago, running an illegal, unconstitutional, immoral war from the basement of the White House. He was such an adept liar, because he believed that only his group was right. Congress was wrong, the majority of the formerly sovereign American people were wrong, and lies to thwart the will of the misguided people were justified. He became a viable candidate for that same Congress that he lied to, but failed to win election. Current leaders in Congress, both House and Senate, as well as the acting president, are all Fundamentalist Protestants or Catholics, with a serious plan to change this country drastically. The wall of separation between church and state is especially vulnerable.

Fundamentalist Jews, Fundamentalist Muslims, Fundamentalist Roman Catholics, and Fundamentalist Protestants are very much like each other in essential points. These leap to mind:

[1] They all favor, and practice, the oppression of women, treating them as property.

[2] They all use censorship without apology.

[3] They are all committed to violence, calling it Holy War.

[4] They all confront problems with fanatical closed-minded simple-minded zeal.

[5] They have little concern for ethical questions of fairness,

or legality, or truth, much less universal love and good will. They tend to be harsh, cruel, unrelenting and mean.

[6] They all display the conviction that one's own group is right, hating "heretics" as much or more than outright unwashed unbelievers.

The name "Fundamentalism" was first used among Protestants and is a misnomer. The groups that broke away from the standard-brand Protestant denominations more than seventy years ago rallied around five "fundamental" doctrines:

[1] Verbal inspiration of the Bible and Biblical inerrancy,

[2] The Virgin Birth of Christ,

[3] The Penal-substitutionary Atonement,

[4] The Bodily Resurrection of Jesus,

[5] The Last Judgment and Literal End of the World.

None of these doctrines is really fundamental. Rather more important are truth and trustworthiness, "justice, mercy and faith," *"faith, hope and love—and the greatest of these is love."*

An understanding of mythology helps clarify greatly these five doctrines of the Protestant Fundamentalists. They are pretending that it is not myth that they are dealing with, but rather historical fact. If someone suggests that it can't be fact, because it is preposterous and impossible, they reply that it is miracle. The greater the absurdity the more imperative that it be believed. As their position becomes more and more ridiculous, they become more and more shrill, insisting that "God" himself inspired every word of the Bible, as it is, and that it contains no "errors."

Logical questions for intelligent discussion do no good. "You mean the gastric juices of the whale failed to function? And what was Jonah breathing?"

"Do not mock! It was a miracle, God's miracle. God can do anything."

You can't argue with such people. They aren't listening. "It didn't take six days. It took several billion years and is still in process. In the earlier stages there was no such thing as what we call a day, with the earth spinning on its axis in the vicinity of the sun." They simply aren't listening.

If you don't believe it the way they believe it, interpreting very obscure passages of apocalyptic material exactly as they spell it out, with Germany and the United States of America and the Union of Soviet Socialist Republics and Islam clearly delineated in material written by shepherds two and a half millennia ago—you can't really be a Christian. You are in the snare of the devil, which is another myth! We need to look at the five "fundamental" doctrines.

[1] Verbal Inspiration of the Bible and Biblical Inerrancy. A good serious study of the Bible in the original languages of Greek and Hebrew ought to cure any honest person of the notion of verbal inspiration and absolute inerrancy. Trying to find the original document, which "God" supposedly directly inspired, leads to utter frustration. There are literally hundreds of variant readings in all the oldest manuscripts in existence, and it is absolutely impossible to say which variant reading is the inspired and inerrant one. Also, the differences in style, from one author to another, make perfect sense, if the Bible is a human book, but no sense at all, if it is a perfectly inerrant book dictated by a perfect Divine Being to a series of stenographers who made no mistakes.

This appeal to reason does no good, when trying to discuss this with a fundamentalist. Any reference to expertise in the area of mythology counts for nothing. "God said it. I believe it. That settles it." That's a bumper sticker which does not clear up what "it" is, but does indicate how some minds work, or don't work.

Long after having discarded, or outgrown, the notion of verbal inspiration, I nevertheless find myself, as a writer, held sometimes in the grip of the Muse, an old Greek myth. I feel caught by the scruff of the neck, and amid pressures to do a hundred other things, she insists, "Sit thee down, right now, and write more of this myth-and-mortality stuff." She does not dictate, word-by-word, to me, but when I obey her, words flow irresistibly and purposefully out of the end of my pen, often as fast as I can scribble, trying to keep up with my train of thought.

Where does it come from? I don't know. I doubt if Luke or John knew either. It is a mystery, to which the notion of "verbal inspiration" does not do justice. And, anyway, the people who thought up that notion meant the King James Authorized Version of 1611, in English, not Luke and John in Greek and Moses and Jeremiah in Hebrew. This "fundamental doctrine" is even more preposterous than first appears.

[2] The Virgin Birth. This is a common element in all the mystery religions which sprang up as the Roman Empire collapsed. There was considerable competition among those religions for several centuries. Fundamentalists say Christianity won because it was true and God saw to it. Honest doubters suspect that it was the cynical and ruthless use of military power by Constantine and others that won the day. It was no different then than a millennium later, when Christianity replaced Aztec and Toltec and Zapotec beliefs in Central America, not because it was true and they were false, but because the Spaniards ruthlessly slaughtered the educated classes of their native western hemisphere victims.

Virgin birth is a common denominator in all those mystery religions. The Savior/Hero was a semi-divine being. At the deepest psychological level the virgin can represent pure potential, all the unrealized future, all the unmanifested possibilities. Out of that Source the new Hero comes to challenge Hold-Fast. There are some notions worth pondering here in the myths. But the fundamentalists miss the point of all that, denying that it is myth at all and making it a test of your credulity instead. They keep alive the medieval hostility toward sex and women by maintaining that the myth must be taken literally. It becomes an attack, or at best a down-grading, of sexuality itself, and then a bottomless source of guilt, since hormones function in spite of theology and clerical decrees.

[3] The Penal-substitutionary Atonement. Atonement theories are trying to answer the question, "How does Jesus' dying on the cross save people?" Insistence on this particular theory of the atonement ignores several other perfectly fine theories, and once again tries to cram a large and many-faceted idea into a very narrow straight-jacket.

The theory which the fundamentalists insist is the only true one says that God is bent on punishing someone, because of "sin," which is taken to be identical to crime. The theory says Jesus took the rap, and God inflicted the required capital punishment on him. This theory expresses well the tendency of fundamentalists toward legalism, rules, punishment, severity. The theory itself is both illegal and immoral, undermining justice and opening what would be called in current legal jargon a huge loophole. The judge is showing favoritism. No legal system outside of Texas would tolerate such blatant injustice—to deliberately and knowingly condemn the wrong person.

There are other theories of the atonement, such as the moral influence theory which emphasizes God's love, but fundamentalists have no time for that. Love has never been at the top of their list of virtues.

[4] The Bodily Resurrection of Jesus, and **[5] The Last Judgment and Literal End of the World**. The bodily resurrection and the last judgment will require our detailed attention later in this Chapter, under "Reward" and "Resurrection/Rebirth." It is enough now to note that we need not take them literally, which is a good thing, since doing so changes the myth into something grotesque and ridiculous.

Fundamentalists are opposed to the very notion of myth, as much as are the modern "scientific" materialists. It is because they are really idolaters. In a remarkable study of myth, **The Time Falling Bodies Take to Light**, William Irwin Thompson states it clearly:

> The materialist sees myth as superstitious gibberish from the old days before we had science and technology. The idolater takes the myth literally.
>
> Both are interested in power. The materialist wants to dominate nature with his culture, and to dominate feeling with reason, for he is interested in control.
>
> The idolater is also interested in control, but he wants to dominate the psychic with his ego. He wants a genie in a bottle to grant him his every wish. He wants a world of magic powers.

His idol is "God." "God will punish them. God will get me what I want. God will protect me. God will prove I'm right." "God," in this view, is like a kind of secret weapon that most people don't have, poor stupid, wicked sinners that they are. It is an incredibly infantile and ego-centered view of life.

The main trouble with fundamentalism, far worse than its demanding that we say we believe the utterly preposterous, is that it is mean of spirit. It is a system of beliefs which encourages people to believe that they and God constitute the good guys, the good side in a great struggle. They then tend to believe that they can do no wrong in defense of that supposed "good." It is pure ego, pure selfishness.

Fundamentalists, too easily, resort to lying and then murdering in the name of "God." Since logic was thrown out long ago, and love, too, there's no way to appeal to them to bring them to their senses. They are obsessed with "God," and that God of theirs is cruel, ruthless, heartless, bloody. It is war thinking. They tend to be pro-war people. Their songs and prayers are full of military imagery. They use war analogies to explain things. They pick up some of this from our militarized culture, to be sure, but it is native to their belief system at the same time.

For fundamentalists there is no over-arching Truth, no Cosmic Ethical Source. The word "God" could refer to precisely that, for some thoughtful people, but the fundamentalists have limited "God" to a secret weapon for use in their paltry fights. There is no sensitivity regarding what it would be like to be the other guy—a black person, a poor person, a battered woman, an Asian, a communist, a dolphin, a Martian.

I doubt that Jesus would recognize them as connected to him in any way. *"Why do you call me, 'Lord, Lord!' and not do what I say?"* What he said was, *"Love one another. Love your neighbor. Love your enemies."* The white-supremacy, capital punishment, sexist, anti-welfare, pro-war, we're-the-best nonsense is a parody of what the texts say the fundamental heart of Christianity should be.

The meaning of the myths of judgment do not help a fundamentalist at this point. Instead of leading a thoughtful person to examine his life and make it worth living, these stories tend to put him in a smug group. After death he'll go to be with God, in the bosom of Abraham, on the other side of that great gulf fixed. There he'll feel separated and superior—among the sheep despising the goats, with the saved looking down on the lost. He tends to act superior, rather than humbled by the mysteries of grace and forgiveness. The fundamentalists miss the point of the "gospel," which means "good news," and then dare to call their little ego-riddled beliefs "fundamental."

There is an explanation for what happened to them. They have become stuck half-way through a process which was intended to change them, and all of us. Joseph Campbell tells it plainly in **Hero with a Thousand Faces**.

Totem, tribal, racial, and aggressively missionizing cults represent only partial solutions to the psychological problem of subduing hate by love; they are only partially initiate. Ego is not annihilated in them; rather, it is enlarged; instead of thinking only of himself, the individual becomes dedicated to the whole of his society. The rest of the world meanwhile [that is to say, by far the greater portion of mankind] is left outside the sphere of his sympathy and protection because outside the sphere of the protection of his god. And there takes place, then, that dramatic divorce of the two principles of love and hate which the pages of history so bountifully illustrate. Instead of clearing his own heart the zealot tries to clear the world. The laws of the City of God are applied only to his in-group [tribe, church, nation, class, or what not] while the fire of a perpetual holy war is hurled [with good conscience, and indeed a sense of pious service] against whatever uncircumcised, barbarian, heathen, "native" or alien people happens to occupy the position of neighbor.

My experience in a fundamentalist group in my youth leads me to be hopeful about individuals. One can become unstuck, and go on through that process. I am especially hopeful about young ones who are not inherently mean-hearted. I'm willing to predict that they'll become sick of all the hatred and the violence, and proceed on toward maturity.

As for the leaders of the fundamentalist movement I am less hopeful. I do not believe that they really believe the things they say and preach on television. I suspect that they do not believe much of anything, except perhaps that they are superior to others. I do not believe it is possible to hold inside the same brain their supposed belief in a Just and Judging God, and the knowledge of what they've come to stand for: war, gang-rape, mass murder, obliteration napalm and phosphorous anti-personnel bombing, assassination, lies, lies, lies. The two don't fit together. I conclude that they do not really believe in a just God at all. "Doublethink," as in Orwell's **1984**, is one thing, but this hypocrisy is too much.

è▲

An unfortunate consequence of fundamentalism is that those people who figured it out and left it while still young and active are sometimes so bent on rejecting that mean-hearted nonsense that they feel morally bound to reject all value questions, all belief-systems, all "myth." They will tell you that they don't believe anything at all. I think such persons have a special need to study and work through what they value and what they believe. It should not be left to default. There is a support group available, called "Fundamentalists Anonymous."

A saying in Spanish describes some people: *"No tienen credo."* [They have no belief.] It's not simply that they don't believe anything. It means you can't predict what they'll say or do on the basis of any system of values or beliefs. It says that persons who do not have any kind of thought-out belief tend to be undependable, wishy-washy, unreliable and confused. They may not die gracefully themselves, and they may be little help to you as a friend, when you are dying. Persons who have decided that their formerly-held beliefs are wrong and/or unhelpful need to keep on examining these matters.

Fundamentalism is so appealing because of its quick and easy answers to serious problems that trouble many people. But the belief system is undependable and ego-centered. When mortality looms, it may let people down. Dying is serious business, and ought not to be left to the fundamentalists.

B. Returning Ghosts

What is a human being? "The Machine Stops" dealt with the belief that a human being is a body, which is essentially a machine subject to entropy, and no more. The idea has become widely held in our western culture.

But many persons in our culture can be heard saying, "I have a soul." Persons from eastern cultures traditionally say, "I am a soul, and temporarily have a body, which I will eventually leave behind."

In our case, one wonders who, or what, is saying "I"? Who has a soul? Ego? Is the body speaking, saying that it has a soul? Perhaps the body is saying that its ego *is* its soul. Then what's going to happen at the pending separation of soul and body? Will the body lose its soul? Who, in the Orient, is saying, "I am a soul?" Ego? Or could all this be the ego's way of insisting that it cannot die, that it will survive the dissolution of the body?

The body will disintegrate, just as the machine-stops people say. The question is, 'Will something live on? Is there such a thing, something that lives on?' So far, everybody seems to be agreeing, on the face of it, that the body will not live on. Does a human being consist, at least in part, of "something not the body"? We may call it "soul" or call it "spirit," or call it something else.

Most humans, until lately, have believed something survives, in one form or another. I'm having a little trouble being absolutely certain, as any reader will have noticed. I do believe that ego is as fragile and expendable as the body, but then I'm not sure yet just where that leaves us. Oblivion or Blotto seems like such atypical cosmic waste, in some cases especially. Absorption of individuals into some kind of Life Force or "oversoul" will be worth considering. We'll have to continue the enquiry, before having to decide.

The myth that the person who recently died hangs around in a disembodied yet somehow perceptible state has been widely believed in one form or another by human groups over the ages. It is an old idea. Supposedly it is not commonly held among "modern" people.

Sometimes I wonder. Fair-sized percentages of people say, when asked, that they would not spend the night in a haunted house. An entire genre of fiction and film, called "horror," would not be as popular as it is if no one believed, in some sense, at some level, in the idea of returning ghosts. Horror literature is so popular in our time that it is taking on some of the trappings of a religion, with high priests and initiates who know, and disciples.

So, maybe we still do believe it, somehow. Older cultures regulated their burial customs in such a way as to minimize the creation of these restless spirits who disturb the not yet dead. The unburied or improperly buried, drowning victims, murder victims—there are thousands of variations on this theme. Something comes back because something is unfinished.

Sometimes they come back because they want revenge. At this point it becomes a version of "The Dog in The Manger"—"I'll haunt you to your grave!" Which means, "I'll make your life as miserable as I can until you join me on the other side."

Ghosts that return—who really believes this? Who has had a personal experience of it? I have been watching for it, with no success. I wouldn't want my Dad hanging around, continuing to give orders, as Hamlet's father reportedly did. It's one of the good things about his being gone. Maybe that's not a polite thing to say, about one's own father, but it's true! I have a strong sense of liberation. I no longer have to wonder whether he approves of me and what I am doing, and his ghost is not bothering me.

It seems to me that we live ones already have all we can manage, balancing all the responsibilities and obligations and connections that make up life. We don't need dead people interfering. And anyone who thinks there would be any satisfaction in *being* the ghost who is meddling in what is no longer that person's proper affairs, has an inflated and damaged ego which needs attention now. Such a person would be well-advised to put that sense of self-importance back into a larger perspective. Perhaps seeing one's life in the light of geology and evolution, or even history would help. Or evaluating life from any other angle, rather than always and simply, "Me! me! me! Little, fragile, mortal, doomed and almost, but maybe not quite, insignificant *me!*"

I'm of the firm opinion that ghosts are for kids. It's an infantile set of beliefs, not to be taken seriously. I suspect it is a function of guilt, of one kind or another, which brings us back to religion. I have a theory about it.

The Spirit, or Ghost, that survives and comes back, is a mythologization of the fact of the influence a dead person can have on the living. Perhaps, to put it more strongly, the ghost is a mythologization of the power a no longer living person can continue to have over those who are still living.

If someone dead is still influencing you, you can imagine that that person is right there, active, when in fact, he or she is not. When you have ceased living under that influence, when you have thrown it off, one way or another, then you are no longer tempted to believe that some entity exists to torment you. There is no longer any influence, and thus no entity.

C. Paradise

"You would have thought he died and went to heaven! That look on his face!" We use this notion whenever someone stumbles on pure pleasure. I felt it the first time I tasted honey from my own beehive. I feel it every summer, eating fresh crushed home-grown strawberries on hot buttered baking powder biscuits.

Some have a myth that when we die, we go to Paradise, a place or state, where we will enjoy pure pleasure forever. Often this myth is clouded with the notion of some kind of preliminary test, to see whether you're good enough to qualify to go to Paradise. For many, perhaps most, these hindering qualifications spoil the myth.

The qualifications suggest that our lives and our actions are to be evaluated, or are being evaluated. We'll look at that notion shortly, when we look at "Reward." For now, let's investigate the Paradise myth and its promise of pleasure.

There is little doubt that it contains a great deal of wish-fulfillment motivation. Deprived persons long for food, warmth, love, sex, beauty, or other things, and they want to believe that they'll have all that continually and forever after they pass through this vale of tears and pain and suffering.

It seems a little simple-minded to believe such a notion, really, unless it's taken as a corollary to the idea of perfect justice. Then the wish would be that persons who have suffered unjustly on this side will experience pure pleasure in Paradise.

The catch is, who is teaching this rather strange notion of future pleasure? Through the ages, the persons in charge of things, the owners and operators of everything, have used religion to teach this belief to the people on the bottom of the pile, often while exploiting the efforts of those very people. The previous Pope did it. He went in all his pomp and wealth and told the starving, overworked, teeming masses of the Third World to rejoice in their poverty and to continue to overpopulate their limited resources, because after they die God will reward them for their suffering by letting them into Paradise.

Karl Marx was not being unkind, and he was in no way stretching the truth, when he said, "Religion is the opium of the people." He was referring to this pie in the sky when you die by and by religion and its influence on most of humanity.

The Pope does not have a complete monopoly on this idea. The fundamentalist TV evangelists have the same message—convincing people to impoverish themselves and enrich those very celebrities, because God will pay it all back many times over in Paradise. The arrogance of the "evangelists" is appalling, as they pose as agents of and even stand-ins for Deity. And the gullibility of the deprived is just as astonishing. It's no wonder that Marx became exasperated.

The notion of Paradise is a kind of dope, to keep deprived unhappy people from making too much fuss. But let's take a still closer look at all this. Pure unrelenting pleasure, even on this side of the great divide, ceases to be pleasure. Too many strawberries, too much honey—and my stomach turns away. Almost everyone has a story of how a pleasure was spoiled by over-indulgence.

Paradise will not be appealing, to the sated, or the bored. A Bible story tells it well. The Israelites in the wilderness have been eating miracle food, manna from heaven, but they tire of it.

> *Oh, that we had meat to eat! We remember the fish we ate in Egypt for nothing, the cucumbers, the melons, the leeks, the onions and the garlic; but now our strength is dried up, and there is nothing at all but this manna to look at.* [Numbers 11:4b-6 R.S.V.]

They were slaves in Egypt, so they didn't eat "for nothing." They wearied of magic food and they'll weary of Paradise, too, if they ever find their way in.

The images we have of Paradise are images of indulgent plenty: food, drink, sex, entertainment. There's a silly element in it, too. If sex is bad for priests on this side, how can it be good for them in Paradise? What makes it O.K. there? And if all the pleasures on this side are illegal or immoral or fattening, as I've heard tell, what makes them all right over there?

An interesting footnote to all this turned up recently. The suicide martyrs of the fundamentalist Muslims believe they will have access to "seventy-two virgins," in Paradise. But it seems to be a mistranslation. What is being promised is seventy-two candied dates! And anyway I keep wondering, "What would a body do with seventy-two virgins?"

How much of our sense of pleasure here is derived from the notion that those things which we regard as pleasures are of dubious moral value, and also rare? Carnival, and Octoberfest, and other socially allowed fertility rites suggest that pleasure is associated with special periods when the normal rules are suspended.

Our ideas of vacation, even weekends, indicate the same

notion, that one cannot have rest and pleasure and indulgence all the time. Many people associate pleasure with parties and orgies. Our pleasures are really a form of Time Out, with the clock not running, Time Out from the rigors of The Game. But if there was nothing but Time Out, as in Paradise, it would cease to be a game, and there would be little or no pleasure.

Some older people bump into a crisis upon retirement. Their pleasures, as well as their very reason for being, were tied up in their daily work, and now that it is gone, they are lost, bored and frustrated. Soon they are sick, and then dead. And they do not die looking forward to Paradise, if that means idleness and empty pleasure. Paradise is hardly a myth to die by, for busy and productive persons.

We need to go one step deeper. Paradise—where'd the idea come from? Salvador Dali claimed he could remember being born. *"Fué como si saliera del Paraíso."* [It was as if I was coming out of Paradise.] Could this be a clue? Paradise is the womb. It is safe and warm, and the endorphins are pumped in dependably by Mother. It is pure pleasure. It is not exactly living, but it is pleasure.

So, going to Paradise is going back, back to Mother, back to Eve in the garden of Eden. Back into the womb, where it is safe, and where Someone Else takes care of everything. This is infantile regression, to use technical terms. Is this what we need, to get through dying? "Gee, Mom, I wanta go home."

Mother Church is also a symbol of it. "Hide me, oh, my Savior, hide, 'til the storm of life is past." Life is something to avoid, according to this notion.

There is an even darker side to it. Mother Earth beckons and calls. Come home to Mother Earth. Lie down in the earth, in the grave, in that Womb from which you came. Very few people who use the myth of Paradise think it means the peace and quiet of the grave, but it is a perfectly legitimate use of the symbol.

ა

D. Happy Hunting Grounds

North American natives are credited with bringing this myth concerning the Other Side to the rest of us. It is a step ahead of the Paradise/Pleasure myth of the Old World.

In this picture, we survive Death, and are doing things, doing what it is good to do here, doing more of it without the troubles we have to deal with here. We go to the Happy Hunting Grounds, where there are deer and turkeys to be hunted and taken home to the village and shared with the others, where there is no scarcity, where one's skills and efforts are rewarded.

How could this myth be translated into something meaningful for those of us who are not hunters and gatherers? Sportsmen, so-called, are not what the myth has in mind. They are hunting for pleasure, not their livelihood. They are in no way physically dependent on the lives of the animals they kill. Their Happy Hunting Grounds would be simply the equivalent of the old Paradise/Pleasure-myth.

We have to ask deeper questions. What are we doing now that we would like to do unhindered in freedom and peace forever? Does your daily work qualify? Answering the telephone, making change, talking people out of some of their money, staring at a computer screen and reacting with finger movements, supervising screaming children, making mindless motions inserting tab A into slot B all day long, driving a truck or a tractor, digging in the earth on a farm or in a mine—do you want to do that forever?

The alienation of so many from their work has been noted by thoughtful scholars, and helps account for why this myth has so little appeal for so many. "I'm not doing now what I want to do. I certainly don't want to do it forever and ever after I die! That would be hell!" The Greek myth of Sisyphus, rolling a rock up a hill only to have it roll back down again, over and over—that seems more descriptive of how many feel about their daily work. And Sisyphus is indeed in hell!

What would you like to do unhindered forever? Bake pies? Pick grapes? Paint pictures? Read books? Write books? Perform experiments in order to find out things? There are many activities which I, for one, will feel I haven't done as much as I'd like, and the notion that I could go on doing them after Death is appealing. But "forever" is too long. I don't want to do anything "forever." I like change and variety. I have many interests, too many.

Any happy Happy Hunting Grounds, for me, would include work which "needs doing," ideas which need some stretching to grasp, beauty to create and appreciate, people of some kind to share it all with. It sounds more like what's right here in front of me, which I let get away every day all too often unappreciated.

Religion often takes our attention away from the present with all its dangers and opportunities and responsibilities. It preserves Ego, while letting everything else go. But Heaven, or Hell, is here now, and what shall I do about it, or make of it? What's on the Other Side is Unknown, and the rest is wishing, and misplacing our wish-energy. Meanwhile, what we want, if we let ourselves think about it, is right here and now.

E. Reward

Many have believed that Death opens the path toward a reward. Sometimes it is called a crown, which symbolizes the right to tell other people what to do. In one old song the reward was depicted as stars in the crown, some kind of symbolic decoration and enrichment of the basic reward of power. In another the reward was called simply, "glory."

> Oh, that will be glory for me,
> Glory for me, glory for me...

There is a great deal of "me-me-me" in this.

The reward notion expresses in a somewhat immature way the concept of justice, but unfortunately it is tied to ego. The reward is what makes the old promise of pie in the sky by and by when you die appealing. Martyrs, victims, slaves, oppressed masses—many have gone to their deaths believing that they would be subsequently rewarded.

For this myth to work we need some kind of Cosmic Bookkeeper keeping track of actions and motivations. For many people the notion of "God" amounts to little else—the Entity who must be faced at the gate: "You did this, you didn't do that—so you go here and receive this reward. Next!"

Some people think they believe in a Cosmic Judge, and then they pretend that they can fool him, that they can pull a fast one on him and get away with doing things behind his back. They're like those not-quite-sharp fifth graders, who think the teacher is blind and stupid.

"Does this count, Sir?"

"Every breath you take counts, Kid."

The Pharisaism that Jesus of Nazareth attacked so vigorously had this error at its heart: "You must keep your record clean, and if you do, you will be rewarded." Many tip-toe through life, tentatively and gingerly, afraid to touch anything or try anything for fear some action or experience would hurt their chances for the reward. But life is to be lived, not merely kept track of and kept out of trouble.

Martin Luther cleared this up definitively. He said you can't keep the record clean, and that trying to is egotism. "Sin boldly," he exclaimed, and he's been badly misunderstood for that ever since. He meant to drop the notion of the Cosmic Bookkeeper, and the idea that you will be rewarded for your bland, fearful, do-nothing Goodness. It is all ego; it is infantile, like a greedy child's view of Christmas and birthday. "What will I get? Do I get a present? Is my present better than everybody else's?"

Luther's intent, with all his clear speaking, was to call

attention to the concept of grace, which he believed overrode any Bookkeeper's record of misdeeds. All has been forgiven, he taught, and he really meant everything.

I have found very few people who really believe in grace and forgiveness. I do not myself. Instead, I believe in, or want to become the kind of human being who can believe in, The Undeviating Justice. Not a personal, bribable Bookkeeper, who can be persuaded somehow to change the record, or to pretend that the record isn't what it is, but a Universe in which every action has an equal and opposite reaction, where no matter or energy is created or destroyed. It would be good, I think, to be able to believe that what is is what it is and is the way it must be, because of what it has always been—oh, I admit, it's not an "easy" belief.

I'm fairly certain that forgiveness is too easy. The word is too easy to say, and it's often just a word. It's too easy to say that one offers or accepts forgiveness, and I find it undependable, if not non-existent. "Forgive, and forget. Go on as if it never happened"—but it is not so. No one forgets, and what happened did happen, forever. Apologies change nothing. I find it more true, more in correspondence with how I believe it all really is, to presume that some kind of Undeviating Justice presides over all our doings. But it isn't easy—

Undeviating Justice is a little frightening. Can't there be some special allowance, just for me? Am I really stuck with what I deserve? Are there really no extenuating circumstances? Is it really, to some extent at least, my fault? Is there nothing else to do but *pay*? The Undeviating Justice—it's hard to contemplate it, even, unless Ego has been humbled, the grip on Ego loosened, and the sense of humor aroused.

The Undeviating Justice—just imagine, it really is fair, after all. Many a therapist has enriched himself greatly, telling people that life is not fair. "Who said anything was fair?" they ask. "Go grab yours, now, if you can," they imply.

The Undeviating Justice—"*The judgements of YHWH are*

true and righteous altogether." Lincoln quoted that, balancing the miseries of slavery against the miseries of the Civil War. It all does come out even in the end. Nothing is lost. Your despair is caused by too short a perspective.

The Undeviating Justice—some of us used to console ourselves, cynically, saying, "One hundred million years from now it won't matter." Meaning that what I do today, and what our species does today, won't matter in a hundred million years. But it does all matter. It is all balanced out, in the long run. And The Whole Thing is all right.

I hear sirens in the night. They are gathering the innocent dead, and the guilty. Sometimes the Undeviating Justice does not delay. A lifetime of smoking and you have lung cancer—so no complaining. A lifetime of abusing ethyl alcohol and your liver's shot. So, what's unfair about that? Destroy the ozone layer and some of us get skin cancer. Maybe the "selection" of who gets it feels unfair, but the fact that someone gets it is perfectly fair, and perfectly predictable. This predictability of the physical world is an aspect of the Undeviating Justice.

Some people work themselves to exhaustion all their lives and get nothing, while others are born rich, never work and never contribute anything. "That's not fair!" you say. I say so, too. Let's change it, then. It won't change by itself, maybe, at least not soon enough to seem fair to the sufferers. Everyone who allows that kind of injustice to go on being the case, contributes to it. And yet, it will change. Keep your eye on Iran, on Iraq, on China, on Bolivia, on Honduras, on Indonesia. It is changing, all the time. The Inexorable Forces of History, as Marx and Engels called them, are another expression of the Undeviating Justice.

Some use the phrase "poetic justice" to refer to how things finally work out, at least in some cases. Empires are doomed. Liars find that people don't believe them. Cruel people have trouble making and keeping friends. Idling away time is a less interesting way of spending one's life than working. Winning by cheating is less satisfying than winning by not cheating. Love cannot be forced. There is, after all, some kind of underlying fairness beneath all this confusion.

This myth of the reward can turn really sour, if it dawns on you that the Cosmic Bookkeeper has decided that your bottom line is a negative number. It can spoil the final approach, as I believe it did for my father. He thought he had failed and that his reward would be a good scolding from "God" and then punishment. He thought "God" was disappointed in him.

He was disappointed in himself, and couldn't bring himself to believe really in grace. His attitude appears strangely anachronistic to me just now. How many people guilty of cruelty, prejudice, violent thoughts and actions, feel so smug at the same time about being "God's special favorite chosen people"! And how many seem incapable of feeling guilt at all! We vote for war, poison, rape and murder, and we pay our taxes which supply all that—and we feel very little. How did our feelings become so cauterized? How did we lose the sense of our interconnectedness to everyone else, and our share of the responsibility for what happens?

Maybe my father was wrong about his life, anyway. He wasn't guilty of very much, really. Thoughtlessness, mostly, and immaturity. An immature *old* person is indeed not much fun to be around sometimes, but there are worse crimes. And maybe he did more good than he gave himself credit for. He was more sensitive about his own guilt than many. So his son left the ranks of the Lord of Hosts—was that so bad? And how was that the father's fault? Each one followed the light he had. Whose fault is it when courage is lacking? Is courage something you simply have, or is it something you can muster? Maybe his lack of it wasn't his fault. At any rate, there he was at the end, with a very low opinion of himself, and this antiquated belief in Reward and Punishment after death.

A variation on this theme is the concept of Purgatory. It

began as an acknowledgment that forgiveness of misdeeds or wrong-headedness is not enough to prepare one for "glory" or "paradise." A learning, a purging, some kind of cleansing, some kind of payment, must be included in the process. Purgatory opens up a crack in the idea that we are in a one-time-only hurried, stumbling trip through a confusing maze. It almost amounts to another chance to make up for errors.

The idea of Purgatory has been badly abused throughout history, mainly by the foolish notion that a bishop in Rome can control the process. The thing became a disgusting racket, and I don't suppose anyone really believes in it in this day and age. Again, Martin Luther contributed the final word: "If the Pope really can release souls from Purgatory"—which Luther didn't believe for a minute, nor do I, nor do you—"then, for love's sake, *why doesn't he?* How can that release be linked to some kind of monetary payment to him?"

Yet the idea of Purgatory, when it isn't part of a papal scam, can lead us to another, perhaps useful, myth. Purgatory is a variation on the theme of reincarnation, which we'll look at shortly. The idea is that there are lessons to be learned in life. You will learn them and learn them all, when you are ready. We are all in a school, from which you cannot flunk. Each one will be graduated, gradually, finally. Now that's a notion worth examining. But it's not the same as "reward."

F. Resurrection / Rebirth

The teaching of a literal resurrection of the dead body comes from Christianity. It is another case of taking a myth literally, and spoiling its power to help by making it so hard to believe. At bottom it is preposterous. To say, as has been said, "I believe, because it is absurd," is admirable only if we think our rational powers are a hindrance to our journey.

Jesus rose from the dead on the third day, the story says.

Rationalists have suspected either that he wasn't really dead and that it was a case of resuscitation rather than resurrection, or that the group of disciples suffered some kind of mass hallucination, or that the story is deliberate disinformation.

The pending resurrection of the dead, including those dead for centuries and millennia, is absurd if taken literally. Molecules would have to be reassembled, and one could ask which ones, since they are recycled every seven years while we live, and recycling continues with putrefaction.

Literal believers in resurrection have decreed that cremation is wrong, presumably because that would scatter the molecules too fast and too far, beyond God's ability to reassemble them. Those same teachers and judges burned heretics, intending to extend the punishment beyond the grave, by making them ineligible for the resurrection. How about that for pure unadulterated meanness? And what about predation? Being eaten was another cosmic disaster—again the cynic asks how God will decide where the recycled molecules, which have been part of more than one body, belong in the end. It is utterly ridiculous, really, when taken literally.

The meaning of the myth is something else. It states that the ego, or something very like it, survives, and that it needs a body with which to express itself in the existence that comes after death. Maybe it's not molecules, but pattern, which survives. That's what survives the on-going seven-year cycles we are in the middle of now! Pattern survives, and will be somehow re-embodied, so that the pattern can express itself. That's not exactly preposterous, but it does require a measure of faith to believe it. If one does believe it, it may make crossing over easier. It would seem that it ought to, anyway.

For others, however, the meaning of the resurrection myth is for the middle of this life, not the end. I know how it works personally. I was dead, and am alive again. I intend that statement as a metaphor of the quality of my life, my estimate of its worth. I was dead. I was a zombie and I was brought back, in my case by love. It has changed the quality of my life and the way I experience being alive. If you've never been dead—defeated, lost, cast out, hated, rejected, made hopeless, made worthless—then you won't comprehend what I'm stating here.

Aphrodite is very destructive, and part of what she destroys is pretense, that fragile tower of social appearances. When she came to me, I could not help but adore, but much of my life collapsed at the same time. Aphrodite taught me what resurrection means—I was dead and am alive again. It has little to do, maybe nothing, with physical dying.

Zombies of the World, awake and arise! You have nothing to lose but shrouds and blinders. Resurrection is a myth to *live* by, but you have to die, first—your pretenses, your defenses, your tower, your world, your possessions.

This is the place to consider the rebirth myth, also. Travelers to the edge, that boundary line between life and death, report a tunnel, and a bright light beyond the far opening of that tunnel. It is clearly a birth-canal image. Life is a gestation period. Death is a birth, into something new.

If you're convinced of that, it will surely help when the time comes to go. But meanwhile, the rebirth myth is of great value in the middle of the stage we are in now. Let me report verbatim what persons have told me about their lives. Each of them went through experiences which they compare to dying, and rebirth. This is what Jesus meant by, "Ye must be born again."

E.—"I died. I couldn't even kill myself, I was that worthless. But then I could despise myself no more, and fear no more—that was as bad as that could get, and I went on living, and I came back. I was dead, and am alive again."

O.—"I am very fragile, but I know I am loved. I am learning to love myself. I wanted to die, but now I am alive again, and it is so good, so precious. The little things: a flower, a phone call, the words from a child, 'I love you.'"

B.—"I wasn't anyone. I was not there. No one was in there.

But now there *is* someone in there—me."

H.—"I was a zombie, a walking dead man. I have been dead, with no will, no desire, no interest. Now I am a new man, alive, alive-O."

All of that is metaphor, to be sure, yet it can encourage people. It helps people to transcend ego, and that is the best preparation for the last test. It is no longer "I" that live, but Life expresses itself in me and through me. My living, and then my dying, too, is somehow Its doing, not mine. Dying is not my failure to go on living. Dying is what Life always does at the end of the full expression of itself in a body. I'm glad that what felt like dying back there in the middle of the process wasn't. It was metamorphosis, rebirth. I have been raised from the dead already once. Death seems less fearful on that account.

The myth of the raising of Lazarus from the dead is interesting, not as a demonstration of Jesus' power, which seems to be the point in the text, but with regard to our attitude toward death. Try to imagine what Lazarus himself thought about the whole business. Where was he when Jesus so rudely interrupted him? His body was stinking, his sister Martha stated clearly enough. What did he think of it all? Was he pleased? Do you think he feared Death, after that?

ૐ૱ૐ૱ૐ૱

X

STORIES FROM PHILOSOPHY, WHICH TRANSCEND EGO

The art of dying becomes a study of ego. The myths of the world teach that in the second half of life, the task is to prepare to let go of ego, to "transcend ego." There comes a time, and one need not be a "philosopher," when the perspective lengthens and one can see what life is and where it's going. It's going downhill, it seems, sometimes. But that's from the perspective of ego.

The ego is a function of the brain, a survival mechanism. It operates usefully and valiantly, unless damaged too seriously too early. But as the brain and the organism age, the ego finds itself in an untenable position. Everything is rigged against it. The organism weakens, and falters; the brain itself begins to give way. The ego can lose track of itself—that's the tragedy we used to call "losing one's mind." Or, less seriously, as older folks will tell you, "Your mind plays tricks on you." Nowadays we have more precise and more modern and more frightening names for variations of this inevitable degeneration.

The ego never really had a chance. It wasn't fair to divide the entire cosmos into two parts: the me and the not-me. The two parts are too unequal, in size, in weight, in volume, in age, in life-expectancy, in importance.

Religion is the last collective effort to keep the ego going, after the above truth has been perceived. There will be a miracle, the teaching states, and the ego will be salvaged.

But we can try another tactic. Ego is a function of the doomed brain. But perhaps consciousness is not. There is evidence that consciousness is a function of The Whole Thing. Whenever we escape from ego, through meditation, fasting, near-dying, or altered states, some of which can be induced or forced by certain chemicals, we encounter consciousness. Some want to call this super-consciousness, to distinguish it from the self-awareness we call ego-consciousness.

Both Freud and Jung spoke and wrote of The Unconscious, although what they described did not seem to be lacking in consciousness. What they meant was a type of consciousness which functions below the level of our individual awareness. Some have wanted to call this The Subconscious, rather than The Unconscious. Jung maintained that there was only one sub-consciousness—he called it The Collective Unconscious—and that we all "participate" in the same one.

Eastern philosophies suggest that there is a difference between the Ego and the Self. The Self is the deeper level within, that links us to others and to The Whole Thing. The Self of the World is like the Whole Self, the Self of The Whole Thing. This could be Jung's Collective Unconscious. Liberal Protestant theologians in Jung's own time, and since, have been quick to equate this idea with "God."

I personally find that the word "God" has been too badly contaminated by ego-centered religion to be useful anymore. But I do believe that the trick we are here to learn, in the second half of life especially, is to transfer our loyalty from ego, that outnumbered and outweighed little non-entity, to The Self, to The Whole Thing.

David Darling, in **Zen Physics**, quotes Albert Einstein on this, noting that one's ego-consciousness creates a kind of optical delusion, of being separated from the Whole.

> The delusion is a prison for us, restricting us to our personal desires and to affection for a few persons nearest to us. Our task must be to free ourselves from this prison by widening our circle of compassion to

embrace all living creatures and the whole of nature in
its beauty...   [page 156]

It is worth the trouble to distinguish between religion and
philosophy. Religion allows transfer of loyalty from ego to
another somewhat larger part, but still a part, less than the
whole—a church, a tribe, a nation, an ideology of some
kind—but not to All of it. Philosophy can help us "transcend
ego." There are stories, metaphors, and myths that can help us do
this. They will be helpful to those trying to learn the art of dying.

A. I've Had a Life of My Own

Old persons who have had a rich full life seem to have less
difficulty getting off stage than those who feel cheated or
frustrated or uncompleted.

"I've worked hard, had lots of work to do, knew my duty and
my task, and did them, and now I can say I've had a good life—a
full, rich life, with no regrets. Oh, I made mistakes, blew some
things rather badly, but all in all it was my life and I lived it, and
I'm glad." I know elderly people who talk that way, and I find
them exciting to talk to. They are not depressed, even though
some of them are in pain and others have to chuckle at their
new-found weaknesses. They are used to being busy and they are
very capable people. But they aren't regretting some missed
chance, and they aren't holding some ancient grudge. They lived
life to the full, and now they're facing the next stage open-eyed
and unafraid.

"*I have fought the good fight. I have finished the race. I have
kept the faith.*" A full life prepares one for dying better than a life
missed, or side-stepped, or dumped on someone else. The full
life often involves some larger cause, like freedom for all, or the
right to organize, or the right to choose. Sometimes the cause is
the family and the need for provisions. Persons who kept

themselves busy in something larger than themselves, who preferred to be involved rather than merely entertained, can look back with satisfaction on a full life. There is evidence that when the time comes they tend to have less trouble with dying.

Cynthia's mother is dying a horrible death. She is angry and afraid. She makes unreasonable demands. Briefly she came out of Alzheimer's fog to insist very lucidly that Cynthia *do something* to prevent her dying.

"But I can't!" protested Cynthia.

Her brother told Cynthia, "Well, she's lived a miserable life. Why would you expect her not to die a miserable death?"

When you get old you turn into what you've been all along. If you want to be different than you are, now is the time to change whatever needs changing in whatever way you can. Persons who become old with the feeling of having been cheated by life, of having "missed it," are the ones who die most miserably. What each one can do about one's own pending death is not try to avoid it, or even delay it more than a little, but rather to fill up life to the brim meanwhile, beginning now, if not before.

Rogers and Hammerstein wrote a song for a Broadway play, which contains a remarkable attitude.

> Hello, young lovers, whoever you are,
> I hope your troubles are few.
> All my good wishes go with you tonight,
> I've been in love like you.
>
> Be brave, young lovers, and follow your star,
> Be brave and faithful and true.
> Cling very close to each other tonight,
> I've been in love like you.
>
> I know how it feels to have wings on your heels,
> And to fly down a street in a trance.

You fly down a street on a chance that you'll meet,
And you meet—not really by chance.

Don't cry, young lovers, whatever you do,
Don't cry because I'm alone.
All of my mem'ries are happy tonight,
I've had a love of my own.
I've had a love of my own like yours,
I've had a love of my own.

[The King And I]

She's not jealous, she's not pretending to be scandalized by young love. She's remembering, and being thankful.

"When you're old you're left with the memories." The message to those who are not yet quite "old" is plain: *Now* is the time to have the experiences, if you want good rich memories later. And pay attention, really, now while you're in the middle of the experience, so you can remember it later. The secret of good memory later is good attention now.

Squeeze every drop out of life, now. See to it that your life is full. Time flees, while we fidget. One of the best images in the Bible is the story of how Jacob received the name Israel, which means "wrestling with God." After an all-night wrestling encounter, an angel says to Jacob, *"Let me go, for the day is breaking."* Evidently it was one of those spirits that don't do well except in the dark. You know the kind. And Jacob says, *"I will not let you go, unless you bless me."* Jacob, the Swindling Scoundrel, was the kind who squeezed all the juice out of every confrontation which life presented. [Genesis 32:24-32]

Whatever he was wrestling with, he intended to experience the whole thing.

When it came time to die, Jacob was quite matter-of-fact about that, too. He summoned all his sons, said what he had to say to each one, *"and when Jacob finished charging his sons, he drew up his feet into the bed, and breathed his last, and was gathered to his people,"* and then they buried him according to his instructions. [Genesis 49:28-33]

Those of you who are being told that you're "too old," who are bored with being "retired," which means "put to bed"—try squeezing more in. There are huge tasks that need doing. Don't let the modern prejudice against "volunteer work" befuddle you. Don't do it for the money. Do it because it's fun to do and desperately needs doing. They're already organized—school volunteers, hospital volunteers, nature-trail-building volunteers. There's plenty to do.

A task to do, and the willingness to do it, can take one up to and beyond the brink. The fact that I still have something to do keeps me alive. When it's all done, I'll go on. I'll exit. "When you get it done, you're through!"

Sometimes I suspect the artists have a slight advantage here. Some of them live very long and productive lives, compared to others.

I have this painting to paint.

I have this sculpture to sculpt.

I have this quilt to finish.

I have this poem to write.

I have this novel to rewrite.

I have this double trilogy to belch forth.

We've heard of the idle rich, and the idle poor and the idle young. But sometimes it's the idle old who have the hardest time of it. If all else fails, get a new spiral notebook and begin writing in it, from the front and from the back. From the front write, "What I know, and how I found it out." From the back write, "What I believe, and why I believe it." When you meet yourself in the middle, get another notebook and keep going.

Share what you know. Share what you are. Who says you're finished? Don't quit ahead of time. That may make the exit harder. Let 'em interrupt you while you're busy.

೭ఎ

B. Altruism

A theme in many myths, and a guiding principle in many people's lives even yet, is altruism. Other-ism, it could be called. Doing for others. Finding the meaning of one's own life in concern and work and life-dedication—*for others.*

The idea is in decline, at the moment, and its blatant antithesis is riding high among the power-brokers and in the story-telling media. We are in an age of Me-First and Me-the-Most. Students are up front about it—they want an education so they can qualify for a better position and get more money. There are degrees available in every aspect of business and finance, but no course of study which prepares one to deal with the homeless and the hopeless. The glamour is gone from those thankless tasks, also. Only the true altruists are left, still trying to cope with the problems of others.

They are remarkable people. They have unselfconsciously let go of ego. The people who organized and operate The Storehouse in this city, where broke and homeless people can find food and clothing, impress me as great souls. The people who work in the home for retarded men have some inexhaustible source of energy and willpower which leaves me in awe. When asked, they say that "God" is that source, but I still have to wonder how they can stay so relentlessly at work day and night at such an endless thankless series of tasks.

When people laugh and mock altruism, I become upset. Altruists have something the rest of us lack. And according to my observation they are not afraid of Death. They are glad to be alive, and they spread a feeling of joy with their gifts of food and clothing and friendliness. Death will come as an interruption of worthwhile activity, and if there's any later evaluation, Death will have to do the explaining.

Most of the old tales of Death quote "him" as saying to the

one summoned: "Why didn't you do this? Why did you neglect that? What about this other thing?" But in these cases I'm thinking of, if there is any questioning going on, it'll be the other way: "Why'd you have to interrupt that? Why couldn't you wait a little, until this or that was finished? What's your damned hurry?"

I am deeply moved by the work of people like Hy and Joan Rosner, elderly people themselves, who are busy organizing other senior citizens to do useful work in the world, putting their skills and experiences to good use as teachers and social workers and advisers and counselors. The secret in their plan seems to be to quit thinking of useful activity in terms of a "job," which entails pay and "benefits" and a bunch of other more or less unrelated factors. The important thing is to channel that skill and energy as long as it lasts. The world needs what you know and know how to do. Don't let them put you on the shelf, in the name of a "job." Don't do what you do only for the money—do it because it is deeply satisfying down inside of you, and because it needs to be done. And then let Death interrupt, if and when he insists.

Altruism can be an excellent way to distract a person from preoccupation with ego. "What's in it for me?" may not be the most important question, after all.

Having said that clearly, I must add that I have seen instances in which what looked like altruism was carried too far. In some one-on-one situations, the relationship can become all give on one side and all take on the other. Many a young woman has given up her own life, and any chance for "happiness" and a family of her own, in order to take care of an ailing parent. What looked like a temporary situation went on for decades, and when Death finally brought relief, the young one was old already. This is altruism, too, I suppose. It was certainly a lack of ego which kept that person in position as a servant, unthanked mostly, probably. But is that living—to stay and serve and take abuse, while one's own time and energy dribble away?

In such cases it almost appears that Death came visiting early on and then botched the job. An old verse that wasn't clear for many decades seems to apply: "Let the dead bury the dead." You, come, follow the call to adventure. Sometimes it's a kind of fear that keeps the "altruist" in position, and I must say that looks unhealthy.

Altruism can become the excuse for an unlived life, and when that happens, it is tragic. My mother sacrificed what could have been several years, if anyone can tell about that, really. We expected her to survive our ailing father, and were even looking forward to that situation. She was ten years younger and he was the sick one. But she couldn't preserve herself alive, because of her compulsion to serve him, even after his demands had become ridiculous. So, she sacrificed her widowhood. Maybe she didn't want it. She died at her self-assigned post, having given up ego, using the last of her energy for her task of service.

Years before that, I had perceived my father corrupting the word, "love." When he said, "I love you," I assumed a position of defense, like a football lineman. The words, *"En garde!"* would have been less effective. He used love, used the word, I mean, to line us up, to get us into position to do what he said, to obey. Whenever we refused, he assumed the hang-dog expression of an unloved beaten puppy. Altruists need to be aware of the possible danger that all their giving of themselves may be creating or feeding or aiding and abetting in some way the growth of a monster.

"Greater love hath no man than this, that a man lay down his life for his friends." This is an old comment on the end of the process of altruism. You live for others. You are prepared to die for others. Love motivates the ultimate altruists.

Many a hero risks his life, for others. A man jumps into an ice-caked river to rescue a victim of an airplane crash. A fireman dashes through flames and smoke to rescue a sleeping child. The survivors of this risky behavior become self-conscious when asked by the TV talk-show hostess, "What went through your mind, when you saw that ice? or that smoke?" The answer invariably is, "I didn't think about that. It had to be done, so I did it." Once again, Death, in the sense of personal risk, is not foremost in the doer's mind.

We come back to points that have been made before. Death can remind us that now is the time, a very good time, if we want to do some changing of something in our lives. But, when Death's time comes for us, it'll be easier all around, if we're simply busy doing our task.

C. Transformation

A major vehicle for the older belief system which Christianity replaced in western and northern Europe is a deck of cards called the Tarot. The twenty-two Major Trump cards tell the story of the journey of the soul. We need to take a moment to look at the thirteenth card. This number is widely believed to be a special number, bringing good or bad luck.

The card is labeled "Death." It depicts a skeleton beside a stream, wielding a heavy scythe. Severed hands and feet and heads lie scattered about. Fresh green sprouts appear and a white rose is in full bloom. The sun is rising downstream. In the upper left hand corner is a strange device drawn suspended in the red sky. It looks like a seed, and represents that which transcends, or carries on through, the experience depicted here. In some variant drawings of the card a black skeleton rides a huge black horse. An emperor has fallen and a bishop is praying desperately. A mother weeps as her child opens his arms toward the dark rider. The sun rises between two distant mountains.

The card does not refer to scolding or punishment and it does not signify Blotto. Even though the card is named, "Death," all the lore connected to it says that it means Transformation. The comforting message intended in the card is, "Change is not my enemy." Change cannot be prevented. That Great Change, which is pending for all of us, cannot be avoided. The message here is that we need not dread that change.

Florida Scott Maxwell, in her marvelous book, **The Measure of My Days**, puts this very honestly.

> Age can be dreaded more than death. How many years of vacuity? To what degree of deterioration must I advance? Some want death now, as release from old age, some say they will accept death willingly, but in a few years. I feel the solemnity of death, and the possibility of some form of continuity. Death feels like a friend because it will release us from the deterioration of which we cannot see the end. It is waiting for death that wears us down, and the distaste for what we may become.
>
> All is uncharted and uncertain, we seem to lead the way into the unknown. It can feel as though all our lives we have been caught in absurdly small personalities and circumstances and beliefs. Our accustomed shell cracks here, cracks there, and that tiresomely rigid person we supposed to be ourselves stretches, expands, and with all inhibitions gone, we realize that age is not failure, nor disgrace; though mortifying, we did not invent it. Age forces us to deal with idleness, emptiness, not being needed, not able to do, helplessness just ahead perhaps.

She is more afraid of decrepitude than of death. Her position seems perfectly sensible, and it makes one wonder why so many choose to cling to misery as the end nears. "Change is not my enemy."

The fear that Death is Blotto seems to make many cringe. But Death is not Blotto. Death is a change. The Whole Thing goes on, and on. Only a benighted ego could say that Death is Blotto. Such an ego is thinking of itself as The Only Thing that Matters, as The Whole, and it is no such thing. Death refers to the changes that egos undergo when bodies finally give way.

So, when something dies, what is blotto? That temporary form, only. But that temporary form is always blotto. It is blotto from one minute to the next, every minute—anyway. Death is the last moment this particular temporary form can keep track of, from this angle. But notice, we lose track of plenty, meanwhile. For instance, when a body falls asleep, where is everything the ego calls, "I"?

Some people think that Death makes Life meaningless, but it may be just the contrary. Death brings in an urgency. "If not now, when?" This urgency applies in many aspects of life. Tell her you love her. Perform that act of kindness. Say you're sorry, if you are. Change things!

Just think, how well we can procrastinate, with Death looking over our shoulders all the time! What would we do if there were no Death? We'd do nothing! Nothing at all. If there were no Death, no inexorable change, it would all come to a stop. Everything would become static, dull and really meaningless. We'd stagnate, vegetate, procrastinate and delay for ever and ever. If there were no Death, we'd be as good as dead—anyway!

"The last enemy to be destroyed is Death," the Book says. Don't believe it. Death is no enemy. Change is not my enemy. Death turns the Wheel. And Death is in no danger of being destroyed. Forget that. Perhaps Enmity can be destroyed. Now there's something. It would be worth our while to work on *that*.

Strange Interlude, a play by Eugene O'Neill, was shown in its entirety on TV. After many hours in which half a dozen people torment each other with demands for happiness, and excuses and justifications for cruel, ego-centered immature behavior, Nina, the female protagonist, says, "Our human lives are a strange interlude in the cosmic light show of God the Father."

Her sentence is an echo, garbled, of the affirmation of an advanced Adept from that Tarot tradition: "I look forward with confidence to the perfect realization of the Eternal Splendor of the Limitless Light."

Nina is pure ego, defeated by time and weariness. There is no acceptance and no triumph in her creed. There is nothing to justify the effort and the pain and the enduring of the hours and the years and the decades which constituted her strange interlude.

The occult teaching, while a similar observation, is a marked contrast. "The perfect realization of the Eternal Splendor of the Limitless Light" may well indicate that one little happiness-demanding ego is of paltry significance. We have noted that the task of life, especially the second half, for humans, is to transcend ego, let go of ego, get beyond ego, transfer loyalty from ego to THAT which overarches all egos and all things, THAT which Nina ironically and misleadingly calls "God the Father." An individual can transfer his heart's loyalty from his whimpering little ego to THAT. Indeed he must, somehow. Dying forces it. The death of all our private, ego-centered hopes forces it.

It is unfortunate that the phrase, "God the Father," is still so widely used to refer to THAT, because it is thus erroneously connected in human minds to mythical patriarchal values, some of which are ridiculous and some of which are very oppressive. THAT is not a male Maker/Sire/Ruler. THAT is What There Is, The Whole Thing.

John Calvin, absolutely unequaled as apologist for the patriarchal "God," nevertheless asked the correct question: "Are you willing to be damned to the Glory of God?" Clearly the implication is that if you aren't, you're still clinging to ego, and are liable to the tortures required to free you from ego.

The occult affirmation puts a positive answer to Calvin's

question: "I look forward with confidence to the perfect realization of the Eternal Splendor of the Limitless Light." My Desire, my allegiance, is to The Whole Thing. The Whole Thing is all right. Whatever IT is up to, with all its time and distance and size and mass and energy—I affirm that it is all right with me. IT has seen fit to produce me, and you. IT is perfectly interconnected to itself. The conflicts and enmities and apparent disasters and tragedies are all contained, all compassed around, all held, somehow, in a larger context.

When ego is truly let go, one can rest, safe in the cosmos. This requires more faith than the standard-brand religions dare ask for. They ask for consent, perhaps credulity. The Great Ones demanded much more, and they show us how. "Are you willing to be lost and annihilate, to the glory of the light show of The Whole Thing?" If so, then you are *not* lost, and almost certainly not quite annihilate.

Our fragile little egos search for happiness, but what is happiness? It isn't obtained by expecting someone else to bring or furnish or give something—as in **Strange Interlude**.

"We'll sacrifice and thus give Sam happiness."

"You promised to give me happiness, but if you ever gave it, it's gone now."

Any happiness which depends on gifts that others must bring is false and fleeting. Happiness worth having comes from a lonely place within, where ego gives way to Self, and Self-worth is then affirmed quietly and unobtrusively.

Egos tend to abuse each other more or less constantly. "Why are you so damned happy?" as if the other one shouldn't be, as if one's happiness depended on someone else's unhappiness or lack of happiness. But the affirmed Self within tends to affirm other Selves likewise, and when two or more can share, happiness is multiplied. Not symbiotic dependence, or the current fads of co-dependence and inter-dependence, but sharing, from a Resource that lies within each, and expresses itself as Eternal Splendor of Limitless Light, as well.

The Self is Eternal. All the changes, some of which my ego thinks it doesn't like, are contained within the vast unimaginable activity of the Self. It is unflappable, undefeatable, inexorable. My ego is doomed, damned to perish. One can grow to the point of saying, "I—which is no longer ego talking, but now is becoming one of myriads of instances of the SELF expressing itself—I ACCEPT THAT. Change is not my enemy."

D. Reincarnation

The belief in reincarnation assumes that each one of us is an entity which survives Death and lives many times, in many bodies. Death is the transfer from one incarnation—which means "in the flesh"—to another. When we examined Purgatory in the myth of "Reward" in the previous chapter, we found the idea that we are in a school from which no one flunks out. We repeat grades, until we learn the lessons. This is an expression of Universalism, the belief that no one, no part, is eternally "lost."

Most humans, and most human cultures through the ages, have assumed some form of belief in reincarnation. In our Western Culture, thanks mostly to the teachings of organized Christianity, the teaching still seems a little bizarre. Some aspects of the teaching are easily subject to ridicule, to be sure. I remember a boy in our class in grade school, who had stumbled across the idea. He told the teacher, and all of us, his view of it. "Does that mean that I shouldn't step on a grasshopper, because it could be my grandfather? That's stupid!" he exclaimed. The teacher had no idea what to say, so the child's view of it carried the day.

Extreme interpretations of reincarnation can lead to what some would call an exaggerated form of reverence for life. My classmate and all the rest of us, being good red-blooded North American kids, were very far from such a view. We swatted flies and we shot rabbits and we ate any kind of meat that came along.

The cows that run loose in India, and the sect that wears face masks in case a gnat should be caught in the human breathing apparatus, were far removed from our daily experience. We matured into a culture which sets aside over four hundred fifty billion dollars a year for irreverence for life, so it's not surprising that we allowed the notion of reincarnation to be dismissed as "stupid."

Reincarnation, along with astrology and numerology, enjoys a kind of faddish revival in our time among ex-Christians. Some of it is false-sounding. Nine out of ten seem to remember being an Egyptian princess in an earlier life. What about the millions of pyramid-building slaves, or Chinese coolies? Why doesn't anybody remember being one of them?

Eastern cultures have taken reincarnation quite for granted, for ages. It is interesting to note that those people who are taught it in a way that we westerners are not, find themselves longing for release from the endless weary round of rebirths. They want off the Wheel. In contrast, we who have been taking for granted that you only get to go around once in life, cast longing eyes on the notion of another chance, or repeated chances. Neither group is quite satisfied with the given doctrine.

The world-weary cynic asked the all-knowing Sage how many more incarnations he had to pass through. "You have ten more rounds," the wise one said.

"Oh! That many! Oh, woe!" the inquirer cried.

The reckless life-loving fool asked the Sage the same question. "You have ten million more rounds," the wise one said. "Oh! Is that all?" the inquirer cried.

Some misunderstand Nirvana, making once again the mistake of taking a myth literally. "Nirvana" means "without wind," and refers to the vision one has staring into a pool of water. The slightest wind stirs the water, breaking up the images of sky, trees, clouds, and one's own reflection on the surface. Life is like that—we see a jumble of partial, disconnected, moving, rippling, vanishing and reappearing images. When there is no wind of deceptive Desire, one can see what underlies the way things are. One can see Something still, unmoved, eternal. Nirvana is an insight, a vision, a flash of Enlightenment.

So many of those eastern tales describe one holy person or another, who, after many lives and extreme asceticism and the wearisome endurance of every possible human experience, finally sheds his body and "enters into Nirvana," where he becomes "weightless, all aware though unthinking, alone yet everywhere, without individual character, personality, quality or definition." Joseph Campbell describes this in detail in **Oriental Mythology**, p. 240.

It sounds very much like what so many fear may be the worst of all the possibilities that confront us after Death, namely Nothing. Blotto, after all, after all that trouble. "When you're dead, you're dead." After all that effort to perfect himself, the holy man enters the realm of Non-Being, which is exactly what so many of us are afraid we're going to do, just by stepping off the curb into city traffic.

I want to bring this myth back from the brink, and let it be an idea which can have a powerfully beneficial effect now in the middle of life. I have, from time to time, been allowed a glimmer of enlightenment. I have seen THAT, which underlies all the confusing rush of images and forms. Words fail me, the new insight is hard to share, and it seems to have very little to do with "getting ahead in life," or "earning a living," but I have glimpsed it, and it does me good. Calms me. Helps me "cool it."

A Zen koan hints at this, I think. "What does one do before enlightenment?" "Chop wood and carry water." "What does one do after enlightenment?" "Chop wood and carry water."

So, what about reincarnation? It may be hard to "prove," from this side of that door. But I have found myself strongly and deeply impressed by the amassed heap of evidence, no one shred of which is quite fully convincing by itself. My questioning and doubting mind has been stalled a little, but I'm willing to proceed "as if," just as all serious scientists now do with evolution. I have come to agree with Joseph Campbell, who said that reincarnation is "the best myth we have going."

The parallel to evolution is quite intriguing. I was brought up believing that the Bible had been written by the finger of God. So when I arrived in Dr. Beverly Kunkle's biology class at Lafayette College in 1950, I constituted a good test case for whether or not evolution could be proved. Evolution seemed incompatible with belief in the Bible, which states that God created the world in six days, not very long ago.

The listed pieces of evidence for evolution, no one of which could do it alone, did finally convince me: paleontology, embryology, anatomy, animal husbandry, hybrid plant development, and on and on. My sense of truth was persuaded, and I had to take a fresh, sharper look at the Bible, which I did. The concept of mythology became the clue, for me. The Bible is myth, not scientific fact.

For a long time I found myself attracted to the idea of reincarnation, intrigued by it, and a little fearful of being tricked by my own "will to believe." I do not want to govern my life by wishful thinking, not anymore, not at this stage. I wrote a full-length novel in which the plot moves because of reincarnation—the protagonists have inherited memories from past lives that affect their lives now. I called it, **Souls and Cells Remember: A Love Story**. Writing it was a good thing, for me and others, I'm quite convinced, but I am still not in possession of "proof."

I made a list of the most salient arguments for reincarnation, just as Dr. Kunkle did on the blackboard for evolution so long ago.

[1] The first argument is in reply to the orthodox Christian teaching, that an immortal soul is created at the moment of

conception and survives forever and ever. Logic would dictate that something cannot be immortal in one time-direction only. It would be like being half-immortal. The technical, philosophical way of putting it, ages ago, was, "What is incorruptible must be ungenerable." So, if an immortal soul is what each one of us is, then it must have existed, in some form or other, before conception. This allows for the possible existence of such a soul in previous incarnations.

[2] The world we are in, the life we are living, and the universe we can observe, are all characterized by rotation, cycles, repetition, returning, roundness. Reincarnation says that what we are, at the core, also participates in these cycles and repetitions. We also return.

[3] Observers of children, especially parents watching their offspring and comparing them, find unaccountable differences in temperament, talent, interest and inclination. One seems to need to learn everything personally and directly, whereas a sibling with virtually the same opportunities and experiences acts as though he had learned all that and mastered all that before. Some come on the scene already wise, as if they had been here before. They come as "old souls." Incidentally, acculturation, especially school, wipes this away, whatever it is. It is most observable early on.

[4] Some people, not all, claim to have personal memories which cannot be from "this life." Those who don't have such memories have no difficulty pooh-poohing them. Those who do have them continue to have them, regardless of the pooh-poohing.

I have had "memories," vivid in childhood, which seem to indicate that I had previously been a native of North America. When I came west, for the first time, as a adult, it felt uncannily like coming home. When I wrote the reincarnation novel, the male protagonist was the last Susquehannock who went west to get away from Yellowhair, and now I can no longer distinguish those unaccountable "memories" from the imagination which was pumped up in order to create the novel. "I dreamt I was a butterfly, and now I can't tell if I'm a man who dreamt he was a butterfly, or a butterfly now dreaming that he's a man."

[5] This does not seem to be a throw-away universe, even though we are temporarily living in a remarkable throw-away culture. Neither matter nor energy can be created or destroyed, only transformed. Consciousness seems to be one of the most significant qualities in the universe. Could there not be some law of the conservation of consciousness? "Consciousness can be neither created nor destroyed, only transformed."

What are we here for? Isn't it to increase the quality and quantity of consciousness? Why amass the skills and all that remarkable knowledge and wisdom that comes from study and experience and memory and perspective? Is it really to no purpose, after all? It would be uncharacteristic of the Cosmos to throw away utterly such an amazing thing as a mature consciousness.

> He never wasted a leaf or a tree,
> Do you think He would squander souls?
>
> —Kipling

The "He" here is a myth/metaphor. The question is, "Does IT waste souls?" And if we don't like the word "souls," let's substitute, "consciousness."

[6] Our brief, tiny, more or less impotent little individual life seems so inadequate to express and give utterance to all the potential that is within. Beethoven and Dostoyevsky reveal how much more there is in us than most of us succeed in expressing. Does the rest go to waste forever? I find myself wanting another chance to develop some of the untapped potential I know is in there, to try some of the many roads not taken.

[7] If the cosmos is just, if there is such a thing as The Undeviating Justice, reincarnation, for some, helps explain two problems, one at each end of some individual lives. How can we

account for the fact that some start with such astounding disadvantages? Consider poverty, a rapist father guilty of incest, a hare-lip, and a drug addiction acquired *in utero.* It may be easier simply to decide that the Cosmos is *not* fair, as many assert, and be done with it. Believers in reincarnation have dared suggest that their theory will help here. Everything that happens is "karma," deserved and just. I admit to being not quite convinced. Furthermore I am so awed and dumbstruck in the face of the disadvantages that some are required to start with, that if reincarnation is going to be used to mean that it's all the fault of those pathetic little babies themselves, because of something they did in a previous life, and that you and I are under no obligation to help them, then I suspect that this teaching of reincarnation is wrong.

At the other end of the story, there are cases of cruel, smug destroyers of other people's lives, who have lived in comfort and died popular and happy. Where's the justice? Blotto for them will not be justice. Eternal conscious torment for them in the lake of fire would not be exactly justice either, maybe, and we don't believe there is any such thing anyway. Reparation and change from within would be justice. Reincarnation could allow for that, somehow, with forever in which to work it out.

I wonder why some of us so much want the Universe to be just. Is it Revenge? Tidiness? An insistence that it all not be totally without purpose?

[8] Believers in reincarnation tend to believe in love, and to be lovers. Attraction is a force in the Cosmos. Love is a value in the lives of most, if not all. These lovers want to believe that love is stronger than Death. Maybe it's additional wishful thinking. If so, I plead guilty. If people of good will, the Givers of the world, are simply made fools of forever by the powerful ones who slaughter them all the day long, then it's a crappy universe.

If love and justice never prevail, that says something about the Universe itself. Some people whom I know and respect, then, end up being more just and more loving than the Universe itself is. Where did they come from? Did the Universe not produce them? Why do I admire them, if they're only losers? What convinces me deep down here that they are right, in spite of appearances? Or if they're not right, that they ought to be? If that's wishful thinking, we need more of it.

[9] Conversations with persons already totally convinced of the reality of reincarnation bring out ideas which are interesting and thought-provoking, even though one notion sometimes contradicts another. For example, one says, "I think our lives are so frenetic, so full of hurry and tension, because we're forced to come back too soon, before we're fully rested, or whatever. We must come too soon because of the pressure of the population explosion." This implies a limited number of souls, which must be recycled too soon, without rest.

Another person, not known to the first speaker, not speaking at the same occasion, says, "Earth, with all its tension and conflict, is a great school for souls. They are standing in line waiting for a chance to incarnate. You are so intent on getting more done this time, because you can sense that it might be quite a while before you get another chance."

Another says, "I am no longer 'young,' and I wonder what that means exactly. I find myself looking at life, life itself, from a longer perspective. I am pondering the likelihood that we are required by the cosmic fact of reincarnation to look at life, to experience it, from many perspectives. It's not only a good idea to try by means of empathy and imagination to walk in the other fellow's moccasins; it's a requirement that we cannot avoid. We will get to try everything, to be each one, to master each role, sooner or later. So, if this is one reincarnation among a purposeful series, let's make the most of it!"

Still another thinks the clue is the difference between old souls and new souls. "Old souls are interested in history, memory, far memory and the older parts of the process. New souls are not. They are interested in themselves almost exclusively. They learn how to advance themselves in the process they are in, but they do not comprehend the process itself really at all. They don't ask what it is, or what it is doing.

"Old souls sense the larger process, with all its painful convolutions. Because they have played many roles, they can identify with other souls in the process, and even with the Process Itself.

"Our nation, and much of the world, happens to be in the hands of new souls at this time. We should be looking for a leader who is an old soul, even though old souls seldom become politicians. We may have to insist on someone, like Cincinnatus in the Roman Republic."

Observation leads me to think that belief in reincarnation does make dying easier for the one dying. Curiosity overcomes fear, the sense of adventure and purpose weighs heavier than the need for rest and respite. One can relax in confidence that The Whole Process is fair, somehow. And one can allow and encourage and rejoice in the full development of one's capacities and skills and powers without holding back for fear of some kind of Disapproving Judge. "Be all that you can be." We need to swipe their slogan, and really make the most of it!

E. Recycling / Absorption

Some persons are able to confront life and death with a confidence based on their understanding of the interdependence of organic forms. "I'll go on living—as part of this tree, or as a stalk of rhubarb!" Often these people instruct their survivors to have the body cremated. "Scatter my ashes over the Pecos Wilderness, in the Sangre de Cristo Mountains." Or, "Scatter my ashes over the ocean." They accept the fact that they will be part of That Great Compost Pile, in the Earth, not in the Sky.

Earth's atmosphere is composed of mostly nitrogen and

oxygen, with 2-3% carbon dioxide, traces of other mostly inert gases and varying amounts of vaporized water. The stuff moves around some, because of temperature and the spin of the earth and the varying amounts of water vapor which we call "humidity."

Some of that movement is in recognizable patterns. Certain kinds of patterned movements have been named in a general way: prevailing westerlies, land breezes, sea breezes, tornadoes, and other things. Certain instances of particular patterns are given specific names: Hurricane Andrew, Hurricane Hazel, Typhoon Cindy. These particular storms are born, have a life which is a journey, and then they die.

We are like that, made of the organic stuff of living material: carbon, oxygen, hydrogen, nitrogen—the same elements that are in the atmosphere, which storms are made of. We are found in patterns which are more complex than storms. Some of the general patterns include trees, mosquitos, fish, humans. The humans, most of them, are given names, like hurricanes. They are born, have a life which is a journey, and then the pattern dissolves and they die, like hurricanes. The stuff remains the same; new patterns take the place of old ones.

There are other older images or metaphors for this awareness which may be helpful. Each life is a tiny flame, which is part of a larger Fire. Each life is a spark. Or each life is a drop of water, taken temporarily from the huge Ocean of Life and destined to return to that ocean. Ancient Stoics used the concept of the oversoul to correspond to that Ocean into which each individual drop will finally return.

Pitirim Sorokin, a Russian-born scholar who taught at Harvard University some decades ago, wrote the following in a personal letter:

> The immortal, divine element which is in every man, will not die with the death of the body, but will return into the ocean of cosmic, supremely divine

energy—often called "God," "Brahman," "Purusha," "Tao," "Divine No Thing," etc.

However, I do not know whether this divine element will dissolve itself in this ocean or will live in it, preserving its own individuality. Personally, I prefer to "dissolve," because the prospect of being forever tied to the individual idiosyncrasies of Sorokin—which bother me even in this life—does not seem to me very attractive.

This is quoted on page 230 of **Reincarnation: an East-West Anthology**, published by The Julian Press, Inc.

I have found it comforting, amid all my ego-centered, problem-solving, realistic/depressed activities and worries and efforts and failures and successes, to remember the following truism: "The Whole Thing is all right." I find I can force myself to take a geological and intergalactic view. The Whole Thing is all right.

Photons, virtual particles, gravitation, osmosis, chemical attraction, erosion, life cycles of stars, the life-urge—or whatever we decide to call it, which is expressing itself in many ways and in many places in a Universe this size—all that is what it is, and I affirm it. I rejoice that it is what it is. THAT, which underlies birth and dying, "Heaven" and precious beautiful little Earth, and all forms—THAT is what it has always been, and, incidentally, it is not endangered by madmen. *We* are endangered by them, but IT is not.

THAT is eternally changing. Death is the Great Change, for individual forms. Often our response to some kind of awareness of that eternal flux is Dread, or Terror. Some children are terrified at the news that the sun is burning itself out. "Well, what are you gonna *do* about it?" they demand, and Daddy laughs uneasily, and feels inside himself a little of that Dread, that Terror. Fear is a normal response to any awareness of that cosmic process, but it need not be the only response. Fear is the ego's response to awareness of its own pending dissolution.

When Bobby Burns spared the mouse whose home his plow had just destroyed, he gave us the famous line:

"The best-laid schemes o' mice and men gang aft agley..."
But the poem concludes:

> Still thou art blest, compared wi' me!
> The present only toucheth thee:
> But och! I backward cast my e'e,
>   on prospects drear!
> An' forward, tho' I canna see,
>   I guess and fear!

We must get past thinking we are essentially ego. It is not an easy task. I believe it is the purpose of philosophy, and not to be neglected, nor left to "experts." Ponder this meditation by Marcus Aurelius, who was not a professional philosopher. He was a full-time general/politician/statesman, and an amateur philosopher. If he hadn't written his **Meditations**, however, and worked diligently on his Stoic philosophy, he'd be forgotten by now, as are those who preceded and succeeded him as Roman Emperors. The philosophy outlasted the Empire, and even though the philosophy is far from "popular" now, it reaches us and touches us. See him transcending ego.

> The time of human life is but a point, and the substance is a flux, and its perceptions dull, and the composition of the body corruptible, and the soul a whirl, and fortune inscrutable and fame a senseless thing.
> In a word, everything which belongs to the body is a flowing stream, and what belongs to the soul a dream and a vapor, and life is a warfare and a stranger's sojourn, and future fame is oblivion. What then is there which can guide a man? One thing and only one,

philosophy.

Now this consists in keeping the divinity within us free from violence and unharmed, superior to pain and pleasure, doing nothing without a purpose, nor yet falsely and with hypocrisy, not feeling the need of another man's doing or not doing something, and furthermore, accepting all that happens and all that is allotted us, as coming from the source, whatever it is; and, finally, waiting for death with a cheerful mind, since it is nothing but a dissolving of the elements of which each living being is composed.

If the elements themselves are not harmed by each continually changing into another, why should a man feel any dread of the change and dissolution of all his elements? For it is as Nature wills it, and nothing is evil which Nature wills.

This discussion, also, must be pulled back from the yawning precipice, that great gulf fixed, in order to see something that can be helpful for life *now*, in the middle of the process. We wonder whether the ego will survive Death. Maybe it doesn't matter really very much. Life will go on. The Whole Thing is all right. Meanwhile, what?

Ponder this:

Many things are hard to believe, and a future life, some say, is quite incredible, and the mere thought of it a sort of madness.... Well, I should myself put the matter rather differently. The present life is incredible, a future credible. To be alive, actually existing, to have emerged from darkness and silence, to be here today is certainly incredible. A philosopher friend of mine could never, he told me, bring himself to believe in his own existence. A future life would be a miracle, and you find it difficult to believe in miracles? I, on the contrary, find it easy. They are to be expected. The starry worlds in time and space, the pageant of life, the processes of growth and reproduction, the instincts of animals, the inventiveness of nature,...they are all utterly unbelievable, miracles piled upon miracles.

This is from W. MacNeill Dixon's, **The Human Situation**, quoted in **Reincarnation: an East-West Anthology**, p. 114. What we are *now* is a miracle. What we are to be is ineffable, as is The Whole Thing.

We come from IT. Not that IT makes us. We *are* IT, somehow. Think of IT as a huge boiling bubbling amorphous blob of stuff, of What There Is. IT is changing, undulating, rotating, dividing and recombining, all the time. Out of IT little bits of stuff, of Itself, bubble up to the surface. The bubbles interact with other nearby bubbles for long or short periods of time, before returning to the blob. The blob is What There IS. And there is One. You are a bubble—a bubble on the blob.

The bubbles are very precious, especially to themselves and sometimes to each other, while they *are*. We are all bubbles from the one blob. Sometimes the blob recognizes itself, in the interaction of the bubbles.

Now there are people who don't like being told that they are bubbles on the blob. That's the ego, objecting. Ego is the problem.

Humor is the answer. The root of humor is spotting the ridiculous pretensions of ego, mine or yours or someone else's. Look at it! So proud! So fragile! So impotent! So unaware, thinking one's own fecal matter did not produce an unpleasant odor! So weak, so barely there at all!

An elephant met a mouse in the woods. "You are the littlest, tiniest, weakest, puniest, most worthless thing I've ever come across!"

The mouse pulled himself up and protested. "Well, I haven't always been this small. I've been *sick!*" Ego yelping again, with all the utterly preposterous explanations and excuses and demands for special consideration.

But, remember this trick. You are not your ego. It isn't really even there. The ego is a mental trick to get you to do things, "to amount to something," which is an old phrase some of us had to grow up with. But now it's time to get past that. Where will you put your allegiance, your loyalty, your devotion? On your own fragile, temporary, imaginary ego? You are an expression of The Whole Thing. IT is doing ITs thing, through you. Your activity, your life, your decisions, your awareness, your knowledge, your wisdom—all are ITs. IT looks at the world, through your eyes. IT comprehends the world, through your mind. You are ITs miracle of self-expression. You *are* IT. And IT is safe. IT is all right. When, you die, you become more obviously than you now appear to be—IT.

Death is made necessary, for each of us, by our being split off from the Primordial Unity. Death is the return to Oneness. Now you won't be a part anymore. You'll be reabsorbed into the All, into the One, into IT.

F. Answers / Perfection

There is a school of philosophy that claims that there is no meaning whatsoever in anything at all. Life, order, growth, pattern, the comprehensibility of the orbits of electrons and planets and of what the honeybees are doing, beauty, playfulness, galaxies, death—they think there is no meaning at all in any of that. They state that nothing has any significance, that there was never really any reason to get excited. They assume that there is nothing there to cause that sense of wonder which makes some of us pause from time to time. For them it is no more remarkable that the Cosmos exists than it would be if it didn't.

That remarkable view is still another myth. I, for myself, find that one harder to accept than many of the others. I suspect this myth is derived from some kind of inner personal despair on the part of the myth-maker, and I feel sorry that persons can live such miserable lives that that kind of meaninglessness comes to be the myth they live and die by.

The Entropy Theory is an idea which certain persons use to express their "realistic" acceptance of their own personal mortality. They're going to die, so they posit the theory that The Whole Thing is likewise, and they seek physical evidence, which they'll assemble into "laws," to support the notion. I suspect that they would say that my rejection of the Entropy Theory as a philosophy of life expresses my personal version of the Denial of Death. I believe, rather, that it expresses my "faith" in The Whole Thing, in life, in intelligence, and in Order. A critic once characterized my writing as "an insistence on optimism and kindness." He didn't mean it as approval, necessarily, but I have learned to accept it as true.

Most humans suspect that meaninglessness is not a myth to live or die by, even those who lack inclination and ambition to pursue the matter much, especially in formal inquiry. We are good at distracting ourselves from the big and important questions. But most suspect that life does mean something, and some have approached Death with a kind of excitement, sharpened by an awareness that they are about to find out.

Goethe cried out, "More light! More light!" and it's not certain whether his last words meant he needed and wanted more light, or that he saw more light as he entered the experience. Kalahari Bushmen dance the Dance of the Great Hunger, which is not a hunger for food, but a hunger for meaning, more meaning. Plato reports that Socrates in the end wanted to die, saying that it was the final fulfillment for a philosopher. Death, he said, would open the door to true knowledge. The Apostle Paul wrote, "Now we see as in a mirror, dimly, but then face to face."

"I'm gonna find out," the old man said with a smile. Everyone is. Some teach that whatever a person believes and expects is what that person will find. Those same persons teach that we are already creating our own reality out of our beliefs and expectations, and they're simply applying that notion to the Great Change.

I suspect the truth is not quite as simple as that—there does seem to be some kind of External Reality confronting us all, which we occasionally have to adapt to. But the idea that we create quite a fair amount of our reality, I find liberating. "You say your life is locked up. Well, who locked it?" a wise teacher asked me once in a serious crisis. And he was perfectly right—I had locked it. I was creating the "problem," which is not quite the same as saying that I had created my own reality, all of it. But what I had done I could quit doing and some of it I could undo, even, so I needed that insight, and benefitted greatly from following it.

"Smile, and the world smiles with you."

"Make the best of it."

"Put the best light you can on it."

"Learn from it."

"Chalk it up to experience."

"It's all copy, for later."

"What you do with it is more important than what it is."

I think all these pieces of wise, and sometimes unwanted, advice for the person who is in some kind of trouble can actually be very helpful.

We can confront Death with such an attitude. Curious, inquisitive persons will be at a slight advantage here. "I'm gonna find out." Persons who tend to take a positive view, and have positive experiences to remember and tell about, have a better advantage. "Death? What happens to you when you die? I don't really know. I'm about to find out. But whatever it is, I accept it. I'll take it! It'll be as good as life was."

Life is a gift. It's all gift. That's the meaning of Grace, which so few really do believe in and trust. Do you believe the Cosmos is a safe place, for you to be in?

The gift of life is short, considered one life at a time. That is simply what it is, short. The question isn't, "Must I give it back?" The question is, "Have I lived it?" And another good question is, "Has my life affirmed the gift which is expressing itself in other lives around me?" All of life is a gift. My life. My wife's life. My friend's life. My granddaughter's life. The lives of people I haven't met yet, but look forward to meeting some day. The living Biosphere Itself.

"For everything, there is a season: A time to live, and a time to die." "Life is a one-way road." Birth, time, growth, time, maturity, time—and then we come to the stage which is the end. It is fitting, at that stage, to use the perspective of long time, to remember, to amass the wisdom, to tidy up things, especially relationships, to get rid of *impedimenta* [baggage, stuff], and to say loving goodbyes. Knowing and accepting, at an earlier stage, that this stage is pending, will create less struggle and resistance, on all sides.

The TV series, **Beauty and the Beast**, presented fascinating doses of mythology to the viewing public. In one episode, Beauty is called to go to Providence. Beast says that Providence means what was intended to happen. Then I break in, in my own living room, and ask, "Intended by whom? What is the source of that intentionality? 'God' is too easy, too glib a non-answer." The program kept going, in spite of my attempted interruption.

Providence comes from "provide." "God will provide," the verse says, but that's still too easy. The way it turns out affects the very process of turning out that we are still in the middle of. It takes faith to believe that, to believe that all these turnings and twistings will "turn out," and that that turning out will be "all right."

Many great spirits have reported, near the end of their lives, that they can see a pattern in it now, looking back, that it all makes a kind of sense, and that it all happened almost inevitably. Persons who believe in Providence, even if "God" is a metaphor, can regard themselves as at home in the Cosmos, dead or alive.

ે&

Our culture, in all its blatant confusion, seems to be telling us that Death is an enemy, an evil to be overcome. Branches of the medical profession, and some new businesses, which offer to freeze you until the Absolute Cure is found, take this attitude toward Death. But when we think about it, we can see that Death is perfectly natural, part of the arrangement of things, and not evil. It is Ego that must be overcome.

Egos often presume to control where they should not. My father was trying to control, to rule the world, his world, all the way down to his next-to-last sentence spoken to me. Death has a way of stopping that. In that sense Death is a comfort. Caligula died. Franco finally died, after decades of Spanish sentences which began, *"Cuando muera Franco..."* [When Franco dies...] The current crop of lying mass-murderers will all die.

We need to understand the concepts of Ego and Self—and transfer loyalty. Am I Ego? No, I am Self. Ego is temporary, useful in making this temporary vehicle functional, but not eternal. The Self is eternal, and I am that. Death immerses me again in THAT. Meditation does so, also, partially, in advance. It does me good to practice that, now, while there is time.

> Be thankful for our death! We can experience meditation at least once a life! And we can get centered. If you would not center yourself happily throughout this life, then you've no alternative but be forced to be centered at least once. But if you do it happily throughout life, through meditation, then when the real time for a final centeredness comes, you are treading familiar territory; you are quite happy.

This is from **Meditation and the Art of Dying**, by Pandit Usharbudh Arya.

The writings of Joseph Campbell can help the reader shift

the focus of his or her true being from ego, which perishes, to THAT from which all temporary forms come and to which they return. The Whole Thing is all right. I am safe in the cosmos.

Moyers: "How can the myths help us through that final passage through the dark gate?"

Campbell: "Well, that is no problem at all. The problem in middle life, when the body has reached its climax of power and begins to decline, is to identify yourself not with the body, which is falling away, but with the consciousness of which it is a vehicle. This is something I learned from the myths. What am I? Am I the bulb that carries the light, or am I the light of which the bulb is the vehicle?

"One of the psychological problems in growing old is the fear of death. People resist the door of death. But the body is a vehicle of consciousness, and if you can identify with the consciousness, you can watch this body go like an old car. There goes the fender, there goes the tire, one thing after another—but it's predictable. And then, gradually, the whole thing drops off, and consciousness rejoins consciousness. It is no longer in this particular environment."

This is from **The Power of Myth**, by Campbell and Moyers, pp. 70-71.

Curiosity and anticipation may cast out fear. We are going to find out!

꿈꿈꿈

XI

WHOSE TASK IS THIS?

In the midst of the houseful that had gathered for my mother's funeral my father cried out from his bed, without preamble, addressing no one in particular, "I thought I'd be dead by now." Another time he called, "Why doesn't God come and take me?" Another time, sweeping his arm to include all in the room, he declared, "I want you all to pray that I die."

I felt annoyance at my father's behest. His dying, he seemed to think, was something someone else was supposed to tend to. It was God's task, primarily. We were supposed to take part by praying. In contrast, I felt it had become my task to give him permission and then "wholly aghast him," by telling him to take up his task and go ahead and die.

My very earliest encounter with Death had to do with Grandmother-Great, my father's grandmother. She turned one hundred, when I was six and a half. She passed her one hundred and first birthday, and then one spring afternoon told her daughter, "Mary, I'm going to bed."

Grandmother-Great *never* took naps, so Aunt Mary knew that was it. The family was summoned. I remember, not yet age eight, being at her bedside that evening. Dad was at the foot of the bed. Grandmother-Great told him, "Harry, I'm going to die."

"Oh, well, don't say that. We don't know that."

I remember wondering to myself, in some kind of little-boy way, "Why is he ducking, pretending and denying?"

The little wrinkled old lady chuckled. "Yes. I'll be dead in the morning." I do not remember how they left it. I do remember my mother telling me the next day, as I came home from school, that Grandmother-Great had died that morning. The old lady knew, I thought. I was in no way frightened or broken up.

A growing number of theologians are beginning to state openly that each individual is, or ought to be able to be, responsible for one's own death. A heavy question begins to insist on our attention. "To what degree can one contribute to the manner of one's own dying?"

Of course, some people cause their own deaths very deliberately. We call it suicide, especially when there is some kind of weapon identifiable, like a gun, or a knife, or a bottle of pills, or a ten-story drop to the sidewalk.

The Roman Catholic Church, and many varieties of Protestant Fundamentalism, have taught their adherents that humans are not in any circumstance to take themselves off the scene deliberately. They teach that suicide, like murder, is a "sin," and that if the murderer is at the same time the victim, then the murderer cannot repent and be forgiven. They teach that "God" gives life, and only "God" can take it away. At the same time those same churches do not condemn war, nuclear weapons or capital punishment, and that fact seems to undercut the preachments about both suicide and murder.

At times it seems that those churches are guilty of unloving behavior. "Maximize suffering," seems to summarize the view. Much of the preaching and the teaching have made people afraid of "God." That fear alone makes it hard for some to contemplate their pending departure. Then those people are being scared further by threats of posthumous divine punishment, if they should muster the courage and succeed in hurrying themselves off the no longer bearable scene. It's a case of mythology exacerbating the problem.

୬

A friend tells of her elderly mother, near ninety, blind, unable to take care of herself, cantankerous, troubled over the fact that she had become the total life's task of her ninety-one-year-old husband, who was infirm himself. One day the old lady startled her daughter with the flat statement, "There ought to be someone who tends to this."

"Tends to this?"

"Not the doctor. Someone else, who would come, and tend to this."

It has become a provocative idea for some of us. "The Tender." It used to be the doctor, back when he was the barber/surgeon, summoned to a bed of pain and weakness. He'd let out a basinful of blood, which was usually enough. And then the priest came to be a kind of "Tender," with his Extreme Unction, those Last Rites. That psychological shove often sufficed, and even his very entrance into the sickroom came to be thought of as "the kiss of death."

The Tender. Not a doctor, the old lady said. All of Jack Kevorkian's problems are caused by the fact that he's a doctor. Could a mythologist do it, carry out the task of the Tender? It should probably not be a clergyman. Some would want pay, and would convert the process into a disgusting racket, as happened before, with other related but not quite identical issues.

The Tender. An act of love, of service, of help. A friend of someone in the family. No organization, no advertising, no credentials. Word of mouth only. The Tender. He has watched the agony. He knows the person dying. He knows what to do . . .

A sensitive young man was interviewed on a TV news program. He is known among the community of people with AIDS as a caring person who is willing to help those who are dying, help them die, that is, with dignity before the absolutely miserable end. He has helped eight people. He is openly guilty of "aiding suicide." He has AIDS himself, and is therefore impervious to legal threats. "What are they going to do—kill me?" He did not appear to be any kind of criminal, even though the interviewer kept referring to the fact that he has done things which are "against the law."

He appeared to be a prototype of The Tender, someone who comes and "tends to this." We marveled at his courage and his gentle reaching out. He stated that he has lost *eighty* close friends, and noted that all his grandparents counted together have not dealt that much and that closely with Death.

Some states have laws on the books which state that suicide is a crime. They seem to have little effect on successful suicides—if a person can defy the churches, as well as the Source of all Love and Power in all the Cosmos, he can defy a bankrupt state.

The laws against "assisted suicide" are much in the news. These laws make it harder and lonelier for the one who is ready to go. He has trouble enlisting aid. And accomplices to the crime of suicide very definitely can get into serious trouble.

My friend's elderly mother had a valuable insight, when she stated that the Tender should not be the doctor. The medical institutions are geared almost entirely toward the opposite emphasis, that Death is to be resisted, and even fought. Or at least that was true until the profit motive replaced altruism as the underpinning of the entire enterprise.

Kevorkian has stated, in the midst of all his legal entanglements, that the problem he confronts is not a medical or a legal problem. "It's mythology! It's all mythology." The fundamentalist prosecutor lost his bid for re-election and his successor threw dozens of cases out, so we can be hopeful. The general public may someday be ready for compassion and good sense, sooner than the legalistic theologians, some of whom have wormed their way into high office when we were not attentive. But meanwhile, Dr. Kevorkian went to jail, finally.

In any case, "doctor-assisted suicide" should be a moot point for discussion, until we set up a single-payer system of health care. Insurance companies, and the profit motive, ought not be part of this debate at all. The current arrangement of things is a shame and a disgrace.

There is a group, formerly called The Hemlock Society, now called Compassion and Choices, which is trying to be helpful through all this. They can in no way be accused of "fomenting suicide." They are concerned solely about persons already caught in a terminal illness, in which pain and expense have become formidable factors. They warn accomplices to be very careful, because of the rampant legal nonsense noted above. They are trying to help enact saner laws.

Compassion and Choices doesn't use the word "suicide." They prefer the term "self-deliverance." They do not want even to seem to be aiding mentally distraught persons who may try to end their lives prematurely. They are there to provide information to persons in the grip of terminal illness, and to begin the task of stirring our society as a whole to think more clearly and more sanely and more humanely about the end of life.

Suicide is not my main concern anyway, in all these considerations. All too often suicide is a tragedy, perhaps really an error, a cry for help gone wrong. Hamlet exposed our cowardice, as he calls it. We think about it, less dramatically than he did, but mostly we can't pull it off, just as he couldn't.

> To be or not to be: that is the question.
> Whether 'tis nobler in the mind to suffer
> The slings and arrows of outrageous fortune,
> Or to take arms against a sea of troubles,
> And by opposing end them? To die; to sleep;
> No more; and by a sleep to say we end
> The heart-ache and the thousand natural shocks
> That flesh is heir to, 'tis a consummation

> Devoutly to be wish'd. To die, to sleep;
> To sleep? perchance to dream. Ay, there's the rub;
> For in that sleep of death what dreams may come
> When we have shuffled off this mortal coil,
> Must give us pause.
> ...the dread of something after death,
> The undiscover'd country from whose bourn
> No traveller returns, puzzles the will
> And makes us rather bear those ills we have
> Than fly to others that we know not of.
> Thus conscience does make cowards of us all;
> And thus the native hue of resolution
> Is sicklied o'er with the pale cast of thought,
> And enterprises of great pitch and moment
> With this regard their currents turn awry,
> And lose the name of action.

Hamlet, who is part of the tradition underlying our culture, really isn't much help.

I suspect that MacBeth's soliloquy, upon learning of his wife's suicide, is better known, or at least more widely believed.

> Tomorrow, and tomorrow, and tomorrow,
> Creeps in this petty pace from day to day
> To the last syllable of recorded time,
> And all our yesterdays have lighted fools
> The way to dusty death. Out, out, brief candle!
> Life's but a walking shadow, a poor player
> That struts and frets his hour upon the stage
> And then is heard no more. It is a tale
> Told by an idiot, full of sound and fury,
> Signifying nothing.

It's a very grim evaluation of family, sunsets, music, laughter, truth-telling and learning, sharing, knowing, caring, loving and being loved. Mostly it's a pose, I suspect. How many people really agree with MacBeth's evaluation of life? How many even of the inmates of those institutions, where we "warehouse" those whose active lives are over, really believe what MacBeth says? If they did, wouldn't they figure out how to hie themselves away?

I'm thinking of something more subtle than simply suicide, assisted or not. To what extent did my mother choose to go when and how she did? She was found sitting on a backless stool, no longer able to take care of her ailing husband and his impossible demands for attention. Death didn't even knock her to the floor. Often, when I'm retelling this, I find myself adding my personal conviction, "She knew what she was doing."

Sometimes, in some sense, the cause of death is self-inflicted, over time, and not in the sense of a short-term weapon-induced suicide. There are years of smoking in thousands of stories—more than a thousand deaths a day—and there are years of drinking far too much, in many a case of exhausted liver. Is that suicide? Perhaps, but not in the conventional sense.

Can selfishness/meanness be called a cause of death? I understand there is evidence to the contrary, from nursing homes for the elderly. The kind and gentle die easily and soon. The mean and cantankerous live on, extending the misery. Isn't there such a thing as victorious dying? Can't there be graceful and gracious goodbyes and then have it over? What purpose is served by resisting and hanging on, with that demanding complaining?

I recall my observation of our friend Bernie's last days. She had not made such a hard thing out of dying. She had never said a nasty thing about anyone, never uttered a hostile word that any of us had ever heard or heard of, never felt superior to other kinds or colors of people, and went through remarkable difficulties early as well as late in life, with a smile.

Her cigarette smoking had resulted in lung cancer. She accepted the justice of that. Chemotherapy moved the cancer from the lungs to the brain. She expressed thanks that there would be little pain. As her brain gave way, she began to call, as if across that great gulf, "Hello! Hello!" She smiled, told the nurses she was fine, cussed a little for the only time in her entire life, because of the frustrations of being unable to express herself as she wanted.

We visited her during those last days. She was like a child—hairless, pleasant, agreeable, obedient, spiritless. She smiled, but was no longer quite herself. I remember thinking, "If she was really a child, my child, I'd be worried about a lack of spunk." She died peacefully one night in her sleep.

Is that the meaning of life? To wear out the spunk? Get rid of that inner fire? They tell me I've always had a lot of it, maybe too much. My mother also did. Are we supposed to let it go out? Put it out? Is that the task facing us?

Can a person will to die? We all know stories of persons who decided to die, and then proceeded to do so. Nothing wrong with them, the stories say, meaning the subsequent dissection didn't reveal the physical "cause" of death. The cause was something else, some lack of on-going will to live. But now I don't mean a lack of will. I mean a deliberate will, to die. As in, "I quit." Or, "I'm a-movin' on."

"He lowered his head and gave up his spirit."

"I now stop fighting. I now deliberately relax. Here I go, down in there, ready, reconciled to—whatever. I hereby *die*."

It is not a loving act to hinder that departure for someone, or to refuse to talk about it, or plan for it. And it is not a loving act to delay one's own departure, by clinging and demanding, and consuming every resource and every ounce of energy from everyone around. The loving thing is to excuse oneself from the scene and go.

All the religions of the world say, one way or another, that something can, and even must, die in advance. "You must be born again," means that. "I die daily," means that. Myths of journeys to the underworld mean that—Persephone, Orpheus, Euridice, Odysseus. "I am crucified with Christ," means that, if it means anything.

"Transcend ego" is our inadequate modern phrase for this. Kill off, more or less deliberately, that which resists dying, that which thinks that this particular fragile arrangement of molecules is of more significance than any or all of the others. Circumstances, especially failures, and a good sense of humor can be helpful in putting this nuisance in its place. The ego, I mean. Persons who have never thought about any of this, who think that their little ego really is superior and special, are the ones caught off guard by Old Death. One can spend some time putting proud little ego in perspective. He is heading for oblivion at last, whether or no.

Some situations that involve dying persons make us think long thoughts. At times little seems to be left except trouble and botheration for other people. It's true that the caregivers can learn many worthwhile things about life and love, but sometimes life is made sour and love's flame is sorely tested, if the misery goes on too long. What can the dying person do to make life better, happier, more instructive, easier, more pleasant, more worth the trouble—for anyone? Can a person sense that usefulness has gone out of one's own life? Can one muster the will-power and say, "That's enough!"? Can one begin now to develop the courage which will be required *then*? I have better questions than I have answers.

My father thought his dying was something someone else had to do. The same idea is inherent in all the talk and thinking about the Tender and assisted suicide. I do not want to be the one telling people I don't know, who are older than I or sicker than I, "Go ahead and die! Get on with it! Get out of the way! Hie yourself off from here!" No. I had that unasked-for task to do with my father. I "wholly aghasted" him. But I do not want to generalize.

What I want is to begin now to prepare myself for what appears to be another task of mine, with reference to myself. And if my sharing these ruminations helps someone else take up a similar task, for himself or herself, that's fine. Whose task *is* this? In my case, I want it to be, at least partly, *mine!* Depending on circumstances, perhaps wholly mine.

I look for insight in the other language I know well. In Spanish, the phrase is *se murió*. What is the effect of the reflexive? It seems to make it even less active than the English, "he died." The reflexive serves as the passive voice, with many verbs. *Se ve* [it is seen]. *Se dice* [it is said]. But here, we could take it as reflexive literally, as if it were something you do *to yourself*, which makes it plenty active. *Se murió!* Not the same as *se mató* [he killed himself], but by no means passive either.

There are many stories floating around, in small circle traditions mostly, it seems, of persons who "died on purpose." Tom Smiley's mother gave up the will to live shortly after her husband died. She was in no way sick, in the modern medical sense. She simply was finished with living, and so died.

A certain king in the Bible turned his face to the wall and did the same thing, but in his case it was out of shame. According to other stories, it can be done for various reasons: weariness, loneliness, rejection of indignity, rejection of pain, rejection of drugs that take away selfhood anyway, or a sense of completeness and completion and readiness for the next adventure, whatever it is.

Our culture is choosing death, what some have called "megadeath," with little difficulty. The military budgets of the governments of all the world indicate this. However, it is still hard for individuals in our culture to choose death. We are powerfully taught not to. In spite of that, many do, but the tendency is to keep those stories quiet.

A couple visited the neighbor's invalid grandmother almost daily, talking to her, pulling her away from the television, reading the classics to her. In the evening they came and carried her outside to see the full moon. They became important in her life, to understate it. Then the neighbor made plans to move, to a better and larger house some distance away, and that would necessarily entail taking Grandmother along. "I don't want to move," she said.

"We'll come visit you, often," her friends promised.

"I don't want to move!" And she didn't. Three days before the scheduled move, she died.

I recall how Mr. Beene, our landlord, died with a kind of surly courage. He almost stopped talking. When asked about it, he growled, "I talk nonsense." He did quit eating. "I don't want to live anymore." And then he died. So it can be done.

Grieving in advance can make this easier, too, I've learned. Being realistic about what we can do for each other, and being frank about our love for each other, now, while everyone is alive and healthy, will make visits by Old Death a little easier. Pathological grief is always guilt, and procrastination is almost always right in the middle of it. "I intended to do this or that—tell him I loved him, go visit, send him a message of what I really felt, say I'm sorry, tell him I no longer held that grudge— but I never dreamed *this* would happen. Now there's no time."

So, now, while there is time, is the time, for love, for saying that you love, for acting as if you loved. "Death is the end of choices," an old teacher of mine said once. I don't know how he knew that for sure, but it looks reasonable enough. *Now* is an opportunity for choices, at any rate. So much of the now-it's-too-late message in Christianity, which turns to meanness in the preaching of some, has this intent, I think. Death does make it too late to do or say much more, whether you're the one dying, or the one being left behind.

Johnnette's grandmother couldn't get along with family, or paid caregivers. She had been hard to get along with forever anyway, so they finally put her in a nursing home. She hated it.

From there she railed at everyone, scaring horribly the little kids who were forced to visit her. "Why don't you shoot me?"

Finally Johnnette said, "Grandma, I'm not going to shoot you. It's *your* life, not mine!"

Now we're getting somewhere. Can we learn to suppose that ending one's life is one's own responsibility, finally? Or at least that it may come to that? Does it need to continue to be so unimaginable, so out of the question, so horrifying? God does *not* come, and take us. We die, or we don't, yet. Or we dally, we delay, even as we say we wish we didn't. "I thought I'd be dead by now." Can dying become something we know we must eventually deliberately *do*?

How rare it is, how noble and loving it is—that a person decides that he or she wants no more of the indignity, the expense, the helplessness, and the uselessness of those stages of advanced weakness that are possible and more and more probable in advanced old age!

A place to start this remythologization process, surely, is with the so-called "heroic measures" taken by the medical establishment. It is one thing to keep a teenager alive with an artificial kidney. Without question, oxygen and blood transfusions can save lives. But when life has already degenerated beyond the useful and the enjoyable, what do these heroic measures save?

Courageous people are forbidding heroic measures in advance, through what is called a "living will." The Society for the Right to Die is publicizing this idea more and more effectively, and offers copies of the proper legal forms. The underlying idea is that when the time comes, the courageous person will lay himself down deliberately, and be gone.

When my son tells me it's time to die, will I shake my head in negation and rejection of the very idea? Will I oppose the absolute necessity, mustering all the will power at my command to resist to the end?

I hereby declare that I want the courage to be able to excuse myself from the scene and be gone. If age and weariness have eroded so much of me away that the resolve is gone, I want someone to have the courage to take me off the scene. I hereby authorize it, and at the same time hope for the wherewithal to do it for myself.

So, I'm saying that in my case, this task is mine. A question comes up. How can one practice the exit? I do not want to end up like my father, or other people I have known. I do not want to let things take their natural course, that is, slide down out of my control.

I want to take arms against a sea of troubles and, by opposing, end them. But I do not want to do that sooner than necessary. Ay, there's the rub! For fear of missing five minutes, or five years, the mistake is made.

Our backyard garden, our winter hearth, our way of relating to each other and to other people, our network of people—all those things conspire to keep me here, nearer and nearer that razor's edge, where a mistake can be made.

I asked my doctor/friend, Bernie's son, to answer a question honestly, and if, "I don't know," was the correct answer, I wanted that. My question was, "Do you know you have Alzheimer's?"

He thought a moment and said, "Yes. There are five years when you know you have Alzheimer's."

I breathed a premature sigh of relief. Since then I have found a new question. "How do you know when to start counting?"

This question is not exactly a matter of age. It is a case of learning how to live, to be more alive, while time is allowed. The question of how to participate in the end itself is an evaluation of one's role in life, of what one is still doing, still capable of doing, still willing and eager and intending to do. I have observed remarkable instances of courage, and love all around, and am convinced that that is the "correct" human response to Death, no matter when he comes. Courage and love are required, and willingness to take on one's own responsibility.

So we come back to our belief systems, our mythology. We

need a mythology first, which we have made personal, before we can hope to sway our institutions and our cultural practices. Humans do die. Each of us will die. Should there be someone "to tend to it"? I'm afraid of that, frankly. Who would choose that someone? What sort would volunteer? It would be better for each of us to learn to take on that responsibility for just one person, that is, oneself.

꿩꿩꿩

BOOK LIST

Freedom from God: Restoring the Sense of Wonder,
   Harry Willson
Myths To Live By, Joseph Campbell
The Denial of Death, Ernest Becker
The American Way of Death, Jessica Mitford
The Hospice Movement, Sandol Stoddard
Ars Moriendi
A Very Easy Death, Simone de Beauvoir
Pilgrim's Progress, John Bunyan
A Practical Guide to Death and Dying, John White
Collapse, Jared Diamond
Hero with a Thousand Faces, Joseph Campbell
No Exit, Jean Paul Sartre
Your God Is Too Small, J. B. Phillips
The Heart of Man, Erich Fromm
Meditation and the Art of Dying, Usharbudh Arya
The Measure of My Days, Florida Scott-Maxwell
Top of the World, Hans Ruesch
The Book, Alan Watts
In God's Name, David Yallop
The Time Falling Bodies Take to Light, William Irwin
   Thompson
1984, George Orwell
Zen Physics, David Darling
Strange Interlude, Eugene O'Neill
Oriental Mythology, Joseph Campbell
Souls and Cells Remember, Harry Willson
Reincarnation: an East-West Anthology, Sylvia Cranston
   and Joseph Head
Meditations, Marcus Aurelius
The Power of Myth, Joseph Campbell and Bill Moyers

ABOUT THE AUTHOR

Harry Willson's formal schooling includes a B.A. in chemistry and math at Lafayette College, Easton, PA, and a Master of Divinity in ancient Mideastern language and literature at Princeton Theological Seminary. He undertook a year of Spanish Studies at the University of Madrid, and holds the *Diploma de Español como Lengua Extranjera* from the University of Salamanca. He learned more by working: truck farming through high school and college in Williamsport, PA, and jackhammering in Lansdale, PA. He served as student pastor at the Presbyterian Church, Hamburg, NJ while in seminary.

In 1958 he moved to New Mexico, where he served as bilingual missionary pastor in Bernalillo, Alameda and Placitas for eight years. He served as Permanent Clerk of the Presbytery of Rio Grande, Chairman of Enlistments and Candidates, Chairman of the Commission on Race, and Moderator of the Presbytery.

In 1966 he left the church, in sorrow and anger, mostly over the Vietnam War. He taught school for ten years, at the Albuquerque Academy and at Sandia Preparatory School.

Over the decades he has been an activist in peace and justice causes, emphasizing in recent years his concern for radioactive dumping in New Mexico. His prolific writings include novels, plays, short stories, satire, articles, essays and "Harry's Rant of the Month" which is published on-line at www.amadorbooks.com.

Willson's keen insight into human nature is intermingled cleverly... revealing both the stupid and the serious, the touching and the absurd, leaving the reader feeling that he has just been exposed to a truth that he has sensed before, but which for the first time is verbalized.
[THE SMALL PRESS REVIEW on **DUKE CITY TALES**]

...No author I've read since John Steinbeck has written with such great love for the world, and such a profound sense of humor.
[J. G. Eccarius on **THIS'LL KILL YA**]

Willson is writing about ideas that can't just be digested over lunchbreak cheeseburgers and then forgotten in the scheduled hectic afternoon of "normality."　　　　[Ben G. Price on **VERMIN**]

Also by Harry Willson

FREEDOM FROM GOD
RESTORING THE SENSE OF WONDER

ISBN-10: 0-938513-33-8   ISBN-13: 978-0-938513-33-9
213 pp. $15.00

A study in candor, a philosophical broadside of profound importance, a guide to personal liberation, an invitation to wonder—a book that links truth-seekers and truth-tellers. If thinking about God went into a black hole in the 60's with "God Is Dead," here's a book that goes all the way into that black hole and comes out the far end—into liberation. The book is the product of a lifetime of thinking and reading. For eight years Willson was a card-carrying "Master of Divinity." He now finds the word "God" too contaminated to be useful, but he still experiences wonder, more than ever.

Former Pastor Willson has written an engaging and unusual account of his own release from the traps of false ideas about God and the self. His theology amounts to no less than a revival of a kind of monism, the assertion that all reality, the whole universe, is one substance. His journey will seem familiar to many agnostics and independent minds, but his account is told with zest and is supported by experience and deep feeling. Highly recommended.   —LIBRARY JOURNAL

Where was Harry Willson when I needed him, exploring the mine fields of systematic theology in seminary? If you, the reader, want answers so you can avoid thinking, especially about god-stuff, don't read **Freedom from God**. *But if you want your mind stimulated, don't delay; read this book!*   —Lee Huebert, minister emeritus
Universalist Assoc. El Paso, TX/Alamogordo, NM

More important than disenchantment validated is his marvelous call to wonder. He reminds us that if there is grace it must be built on nature. And, if there isn't grace, he bravely points to what it means to be deeply human.   —Michael E. Daly, former RC priest
retired professor of Social Ethics at UNM

*I and everyone who reads it will never be the same. **Freedom from God** is at once mind expanding and spine chilling; that's what wonder does. When we view our being in a cosmic, all-inclusive perspective, we are very apt to lose track of where we are. . . . Then, "The only way out is through" becomes a mantra. . . . Willson would persuade us to give ourselves over to The Whole Thing. . . . "All the multiplicity we see and feel around us is made up of interacting interlocking parts which make up One" (page 112). The word 'God' is inappropriate in that context because we cannot strip it of its anthropomorphic connotations.* —Bruce Ferguson, Presbyterian minister, retired

This professor judges the book to be required reading for all clergy in churches, mosques, and synagogues, as well as highly recommended reading for all thinking lay Christians, Jews, and Muslims.
—Fred Sturm, Ph.D., Philosophy Department, UNM

Unsolicited reader responses to
FREEDOM FROM GOD

" . . . erudite work, instructive, stimulating. . . . Your words are like lights shining, attempting to share the sense of wonder with others."

"In my opinion this should be required reading for every freshman college student in the world. Perhaps then, there could be peace in the world."

"Your book helped me embrace freedom and responsibility."

"You expressed your ideas with refreshing simplicity and clarity. Thank you for making me feel less alone in these terrible times."

"God is killing me, in a close to literal sense. . . . Your book is a breath of fresh air. You are actually telling me I get to decide what to do with life!?"

"I recently read FREEDOM FROM GOD, and I can't express how grateful I am to you for writing it! . . . I was moved to tears. . . ."

ABOUT AMADOR PUBLISHERS, LLC

Amador Publishers is a humanist press dedicated to peace, equality, respect for all cultures and preservation of the Biosphere. We specialize in literary fiction, biography, philosophy and social commentary of unique worth and appeal, whether within or without the purview of mainstream publishing.

The current release, MYTH AND MORTALITY: TESTING THE STORIES, epitomizes the honesty, caring, insight and intelligence that characterize the books we select for publication, regardless of genre. In it, as in his previous book, FREEDOM FROM GOD: RESTORING THE SENSE OF WONDER, Harry Willson challenges readers to examine the ideas and beliefs they may have accepted by default, and to make a conscious choice to replace all that breed guilt, hatred and fear with those that bring joy, compassion, and enthusiasm for life.

Since publication of Mr. Willson's first book, DUKE CITY TALES (1986), Amador has published over thirty titles from thirteen authors. Two of our titles are award winners: Tim MacCurdy's CAESAR OF SANTA FE was named Best First Novel, 1991 by Western Writers of America; and HUNGER IN THE FIRST PERSON SINGULAR by Michelle Miller received the New Mexico Press Women's Zia Award for Best Book 1993.

Please visit our web site to learn more about our authors and their books. We welcome your feedback:

AMADOR PUBLISHERS, LLC
P.O. Box 12335
Albuquerque, NM 87195 USA
e-mail: info@amadorbooks.com

www.amadorbooks.com

AMADOR PUBLISHERS
P.O. Box 12335
Albuquerque, NM 87195
e-mail: info@amadorbooks.com
http://www.amadorbooks.com

ORDER BLANK

Quantity   Price
                    Books by Harry Willson

_____ MYTH AND MORTALITY   @ $16.50 = _____
_____ FREEDOM FROM GOD   @ $15.00 = _____
_____ VERMIN   @ $10.00 = _____
_____ THIS'LL KILL YA   @ $ 6.00 = _____
_____ A WORLD FOR THE MEEK   @ $10.00 = _____
_____ SOULS AND CELLS REMEMBER   @ $10.00 = _____
_____ DUKE CITY TALES   @ $10.00 = _____
_____ CHRISTMAS BLUES   @ $15.00 = _____

Additional Books
(*Enter quantity, book title or code, price and total amount.*)

_____ _____ @ $ ____ = _____
_____ _____ @ $ ____ = _____
_____ _____ @ $ ____ = _____
_____ _____ @ $ ____ = _____

Total Enclosed $ _____

Shipping is free on pre-paid orders!

Send to: Name _____

            Address _____

            City, State, Zip_____

Phone/E-mail: _____

MORE BOOKS BY AMADOR PUBLISHERS, LLC

AMERIKA? AMERICA! autobiography by Eva Krutein (**AA** $14.00)
ANCESTRAL NOTES: A FAMILY DREAM JOURNAL
        creative nonfiction by Zelda Leah Gatuskin (**AN** $12.00)
THE CARLOS CHADWICK MYSTERY
        satirical fiction by Gene Bell-Villada (**CCM** $10.00)
CASTLE LARK AND THE TALE THAT STOPPED TIME
        fantasy by Zelda Gatuskin (**CL** $22.00)
CAESAR OF SANTA FE
        historical fiction by Tim MacCurdy (**CSF** $12.00)
CROSSWINDS southwest fiction by Michael Thomas (**CW** $10.00)
FAR FROM THE ANGELS
        historical fiction by Ben Tarver (**FFA** $10.00)
HITLER'S LAST GASP suspense by Manfred Krutein (**HLG** $12.00)
HUNGER IN THE FIRST PERSON SINGULAR
        literary fiction by Michelle Miller (**HSPS** $12.00)
JOURNEY FROM THE KEEP OF BONES
        visionary fiction by Michelle Miller Allen (**JKOB** $20.00)
LITTLE BROWN ROADRUNNER
        children's by Leon Wender (**LBR** $4.00)
PARADISE FOUND, AND LOST
        autobiography by Eva Krutein (**PFL** $11.00)
THE PIANIST WHO LIKED AYN RAND
        short stories by Gene Bell-Villada (**TPW** $14.00)
SILICON VALLEY ESCAPEE poetry by Michael Scofield (**SVE** $15.00)
TIME AND TEMPERATURE
        illustrated collection by Zelda Leah Gatuskin (**T&T** $30.00)
THE TIME DANCER fantasy by Zelda Leah Gatuskin (**TTD** $10.00)
TO DANCE, AFTER THE DOOM
        poetry by David Condit (**TDAD** $5.00)
TWELVE GIFTS southwest recipes by Adela Amador (**12G** $ 4.00)
UNDERCURRENTS: NEW MEXICO STORIES THEN AND NOW
        autobiographical *cuentos* by Adela Amador (**UC** $12.00)
ZELDA'S COSMIC COLORING BOOK
        children's by Zelda Leah Gatuskin (**ZCCB** $4.00)

www.amadorbooks.com